Joyce Appleby on *Thomas Jefferson*
Louis Auchincloss on *Theodore Roosevelt*
Jean H. Baker on *James Buchanan*
H. W. Brands on *Woodrow Wilson*
Alan Brinkley on *John F. Kennedy*
Douglas Brinkley on *Gerald R. Ford*
Josiah Bunting III on *Ulysses S. Grant*
James MacGregor Burns and Susan Dunn on *George Washington*
Charles W. Calhoun on *Benjamin Harrison*
Gail Collins on *William Henry Harrison*
Robert Dallek on *Harry S. Truman*
John W. Dean on *Warren G. Harding*
John Patrick Diggins on *John Adams*
Elizabeth Drew on *Richard M. Nixon*
John S. D. Eisenhower on *Zachary Taylor*
Paul Finkelman on *Millard Fillmore*
Annette Gordon-Reed on *Andrew Johnson*
Henry F. Graff on *Grover Cleveland*
David Greenberg on *Calvin Coolidge*
Gary Hart on *James Monroe*
Michael F. Holt on *Franklin Pierce*
Roy Jenkins on *Franklin Delano Roosevelt*
Zachary Karabell on *Chester Alan Arthur*
Lewis H. Lapham on *William Howard Taft*
William E. Leuchtenburg on *Herbert Hoover*
Gary May on *John Tyler*
George McGovern on *Abraham Lincoln*
Timothy Naftali on *George H. W. Bush*
Charles Peters on *Lyndon B. Johnson*
Kevin Phillips on *William McKinley*
Robert V. Remini on *John Quincy Adams*
Ira Rutkow on *James A. Garfield*
John Seigenthaler on *James K. Polk*
Hans L. Trefousse on *Rutherford B. Hayes*
Tom Wicker on *Dwight D. Eisenhower*
Ted Widmer on *Martin Van Buren*
Sean Wilentz on *Andrew Jackson*
Garry Wills on *James Madison*
Julian Zelizer on *Jimmy Carter*

*Flood Control Politics: The Connecticut River
Valley Problem, 1927–1950*

The Perils of Prosperity, 1914–1932

Franklin D. Roosevelt and the New Deal, 1932–1940

*The LIFE History of the United States:
1933–1945: New Deal and Global War
From 1945: The Great Age of Change*

Franklin D. Roosevelt: A Profile (editor)

The New Deal: A Documentary History (editor)

The Growth of the American Republic
(with Samuel Eliot Morison and Henry Steele Commager)

A Troubled Feast: American Society Since 1945

The Unfinished Century: America Since 1900 (general editor)

Britain and the United States: Four Views to Mark the Silver Jubilee
(with Anthony Quinton, George W. Ball, and David Owen)

A Concise History of the American Republic
(with Samuel Eliot Morison and Henry Steele Commager)

The 1984 Election in Historical Perspective

The 1988 Election in Historical Perspective

*The Supreme Court Reborn:
The Constitutional Revolution in the Age of Roosevelt*

The FDR Years: On Roosevelt and His Legacy

American Places: Encounters with History (editor)

In the Shadow of FDR: From Harry Truman to George W. Bush

*The White House Looks South: Franklin D. Roosevelt,
Harry S. Truman, Lyndon B. Johnson*

Herbert Hoover

William E. Leuchtenburg

Herbert
Hoover

THE AMERICAN PRESIDENTS

ARTHUR M. SCHLESINGER, JR., AND SEAN WILENTZ

GENERAL EDITORS

Times Books

HENRY HOLT AND COMPANY, NEW YORK

Times Books
Henry Holt and Company, LLC
Publishers since 1866
175 Fifth Avenue
New York, New York 10010
www.henryholt.com

Henry Holt® is a registered trademark
of Henry Holt and Company, LLC.

Library of Congress Cataloging-in-Publication Data

Leuchtenburg, William Edward, 1922–
    Herbert Hoover / William E. Leuchtenburg.—1st ed.
        p. cm.—(The American presidents)
    Includes bibliographical references and index.
    ISBN-13: 978-0-8050-6958-7
    ISBN-10: 0-8050-6958-5
    1. Hoover, Herbert, 1874–1964. 2. Presidents—United
States—Biography. 3. United States—Politics and
government—1929–1933. I. Title.
    E802.L48 2009
    973.91'6092—dc22
    [B]   2008026456

Henry Holt books are available for special promotions
and premiums. For details contact: Director, Special Markets.

First Edition 2009

Printed in the United States of America

1 3 5 7 9 10 8 6 4 2

"Writing about Herbert Hoover is like trying to describe the interior of a citadel where every drawbridge is up and every portcullis down."

—GEORGE CREEL

Contents

Editor's Note

THE AMERICAN PRESIDENCY

The president is the central player in the American political order. That would seem to contradict the intentions of the Founding Fathers. Remembering the horrid example of the British monarchy, they invented a separation of powers in order, as Justice Brandeis later put it, "to preclude the exercise of arbitrary power." Accordingly, they divided the government into three allegedly equal and coordinate branches—the executive, the legislative, and the judiciary.

But a system based on the tripartite separation of powers has an inherent tendency toward inertia and stalemate. One of the three branches must take the initiative if the system is to move. The executive branch alone is structurally capable of taking that initiative. The Founders must have sensed this when they accepted Alexander Hamilton's proposition in the Seventieth Federalist that "energy in the executive is a leading character in the definition of good government." They thus envisaged a strong president—but within an equally strong system of constitutional accountability. (The term *imperial presidency* arose in the 1970s to describe the situation when the balance between power and accountability is upset in favor of the executive.)

The American system of self-government thus comes to focus in the presidency—"the vital place of action in the system," as Woodrow Wilson put it. Henry Adams, himself the great-grandson and grandson of presidents as well as the most brilliant of American historians, said that the American president "resembles the commander of a ship at sea. He must have a helm to grasp, a course to steer, a port to seek." The men in the White House (thus far only men, alas) in steering their chosen courses have shaped our destiny as a nation.

Biography offers an easy education in American history, rendering the past more human, more vivid, more intimate, more accessible, more connected to ourselves. Biography reminds us that presidents are not supermen. They are human beings too, worrying about decisions, attending to wives and children, juggling balls in the air, and putting on their pants one leg at a time. Indeed, as Emerson contended, "There is properly no history; only biography."

Presidents serve us as inspirations, and they also serve us as warnings. They provide bad examples as well as good. The nation, the Supreme Court has said, has "no right to expect that it will always have wise and humane rulers, sincerely attached to the principles of the Constitution. Wicked men, ambitious of power, with hatred of liberty and contempt of law, may fill the place once occupied by Washington and Lincoln."

The men in the White House express the ideals and the values, the frailties and the flaws, of the voters who send them there. It is altogether natural that we should want to know more about the virtues and the vices of the fellows we have elected to govern us. As we know more about them, we will know more about ourselves. The French political philosopher Joseph de Maistre said, "Every nation has the government it deserves."

At the start of the twenty-first century, forty-two men have made it to the Oval Office. (George W. Bush is counted our forty-third president, because Grover Cleveland, who served nonconsecutive terms, is counted twice.) Of the parade of presidents, a dozen or so lead the polls periodically conducted by historians and political scientists. What makes a great president?

Great presidents possess, or are possessed by, a vision of an ideal America. Their passion, as they grasp the helm, is to set the ship of state on the right course toward the port they seek. Great presidents also have a deep psychic connection with the needs, anxieties, dreams of people. "I do not believe," said Wilson, "that any man can lead who does not act . . . under the impulse of a profound sympathy with those whom he leads—a sympathy which is insight—an insight which is of the heart rather than of the intellect."

"All of our great presidents," said Franklin D. Roosevelt, "were leaders of thought at a time when certain ideas in the life of the nation had to be clarified." So Washington incarnated the idea of federal union, Jefferson and Jackson the idea of democracy, Lincoln union and freedom, Cleveland rugged honesty. Theodore Roosevelt and Wilson, said FDR, were both "moral leaders, each in his own way and his own time, who used the presidency as a pulpit."

To succeed, presidents not only must have a port to seek but they must convince Congress and the electorate that it is a port worth seeking. Politics in a democracy is ultimately an educational process, an adventure in persuasion and consent. Every president stands in Theodore Roosevelt's bully pulpit.

The greatest presidents in the scholars' rankings, Washington, Lincoln, and Franklin Roosevelt, were leaders who confronted and overcame the republic's greatest crises. Crisis widens presidential opportunities for bold and imaginative action. But it does not guarantee presidential greatness. The crisis of secession did not spur Buchanan or the crisis of depression spur Hoover to creative leadership. Their inadequacies in the face of crisis allowed Lincoln and the second Roosevelt to show the difference individuals make to history. Still, even in the absence of first-order crisis, forceful and persuasive presidents—Jefferson, Jackson, James K. Polk, Theodore Roosevelt, Harry Truman, John F. Kennedy, Ronald Reagan, George W. Bush—are able to impose their own priorities on the country.

The diverse drama of the presidency offers a fascinating set of tales. Biographies of American presidents constitute a chronicle of wisdom and folly, nobility and pettiness, courage and cunning, forth-rightness and deceit, quarrel and consensus. The turmoil perennially swirling around the White House illuminates the heart of the American democracy.

It is the aim of the American Presidents series to present the grand panorama of our chief executives in volumes compact enough for the busy reader, lucid enough for the student, authoritative enough for the scholar. Each volume offers a distillation of character and career. I hope that these lives will give readers some understanding of the pitfalls and potentialities of the presidency and also of the responsibilities of citizenship. Truman's famous sign—"The buck stops here"—tells only half the story. Citizens cannot escape the ultimate responsibility. It is in the voting booth, not on the presidential desk, that the buck finally stops.

—Arthur M. Schlesinger, Jr.

Herbert Hoover

1

The Great Engineer

Little wonder that *David Copperfield* was Herbert Hoover's favorite tale. Like Charles Dickens's hero, Hoover was orphaned at an early age, and, like David too, he had a harsh youth. If none of the men to whom his care was entrusted after his parents' deaths was quite so mean as Mr. Murdstone, his kin were a mirthless lot. His boyhood experiences left Hoover permanently scarred—reclusive and wary to a degree that not even decades of success could erase, and they would have unfortunate political consequences when he sought to lead the nation. Yet Hoover was also a survivor, a young man of grit and pluck determined to make his way in the world.

Herbert Clark Hoover was born on August 10, 1874, in West Branch, a Quaker settlement in Cedar County, Iowa. "Herbert was a sweet baby that first day, round and plump," an aunt later remembered, "and looked about very cordial." His birth took place in a tiny room in a small but immaculate whitewashed gabled cottage on the bank of Wapsinonoc Creek, across an alley from his father Jesse's blacksmith shop.

Descendant of a Swiss family that a century before still went by the name of Huber, Jesse had migrated with his folks by riverboat and covered wagon to the prairie as a child two decades earlier. Though West Branch was not quite a pioneer community, the railroad had reached it only three years before Herbert was born. One uncle drove a stage between two Iowa towns, and another was a U.S. Indian agent to the Osage. Not until Herbert Hoover was twenty-two would he see the country east of the Mississippi. West Branch was churchgoing, sober, Republican. The sole Democrat was the village drunk.

Bertie spent his first years in modest but comfortable circumstances. His father—a clever tinkerer—sold his forge, set up a profitable farm-implements business, moved his family to a larger house, and got elected to the town council. His mother, Huldah Randall Minthorn, born of English stock in a Quaker colony in Ontario, won high regard for her piety, her solicitude for ill neighbors, and her eloquence when she spoke out at Friends meetings. "The spirit," it was said, "moved her beautifully." Bertie also had the companionship of an older brother, Theodore ("Tad"), and a younger sister, Mary ("May").

In retrospect, Hoover sometimes portrayed his childhood as a rural idyll: the "glories of snowy winter, . . . the gathering of apples, the pilgrimage to the river woods." He recollected swimming in the creek, coasting on sleds down Cook's Hill, fishing for sunnies (using "willow poles with a butcher-string line and hooks ten for a dime"), and combing the glacial gravel along the Burlington track for "gems of agate and fossil coral." An Indian boy taught him to shoot prairie chickens with bow and arrow. Christmas treats were walnuts, hickory nuts, "and popcorn balls cemented with sorghum molasses."

For the most part, though, his childhood was as monotone as the drab prairie schooner bonnet his mother habitually wore. "Mine was a Quaker family unwilling . . . to have a youth corrupted with stronger reading than the Bible, the encyclopedia, or those great novels where the hero overcomes the demon rum," Hoover recalled. Pursuit of pleasure was the vice of sinners. An uncle once chided the boy for a grievous breach of decorum: giggling. Secretary of the local branch of the Women's Christian Temperance Union, Huldah enrolled Bertie in a children's prohibitionist association, the Band of

Hope, as well as in the Young People's Prayer Meeting of West Branch, which she founded. She required him to study a chapter of the Bible every day and to record each penny he spent in a diminutive account ledger. Death was an insistent interloper. Bertie himself, when an infant, had been given up for dead. With more innuendo than he may have intended, Hoover was later to describe his early years as "a Montessori school in stark reality."

Quakerism accentuated this somberness: plain speech; plain dress; cold, hard benches. To a degree, the Society of Friends left lasting imprints on Hoover's character and temperament—his self-reliance, his disdain for show, and his capacity for toil—and on his view of the world: his dutiful commitment to good works, his trust in a community of neighbors to sustain the needy, his pursuit of peace, and his conception of "ordered freedom." He did not find it easy, however, to be the son of a woman who was an ordained minister. In his memoirs, Hoover wrote, "Those who are acquainted with the Quaker faith, and who know the primitive furnishing of the Quaker meeting-house, the solemnity of the long hours of meeting awaiting the spirit to move someone, will know the intense repression upon a ten-year-old boy who might not even count his toes." Later, he rebelled. He refused to go to Earlham, a Quaker college; was married by a Roman Catholic priest; served in a war government; and smoked, drank, swore, danced, patronized the theater, and profaned the Sabbath. Of Quakerism, he remarked, "I never worked very hard at it."

When Bertie was six, his universe began to crash around him. His father, only thirty-four, died, leaving, Tad said later, "a void unfillable and unfilled forever." Despite straitened circumstances, Huldah ordered a stone in her husband's memory, only to have the elders tell her it was too ostentatious and must be replaced. (Just once in later years did Hoover allude to those harrowing times. In 1928, when he was a candidate for president of the United States, he explained to an interviewer why he liked food so much: "You see, I was always hungry then.") For his mother, the struggle to survive was remorseless. "You will laugh at my poverty if I tell you I could not scratch up enough to pay my postage," she wrote her family on one occasion, and on another she said, "I will try to do what I can and not neglect the children." But, goodhearted though she was, neglect the children she did. Increasingly absorbed in her religious work, she shunted Bertie off to an uncle in a sod house in distant northwestern Iowa near the South Dakota border and, for a long stretch, to another uncle in Indian Territory. On one of her missions, Huldah became ill, and shortly thereafter the meeting recorded, "the Lord had mercy and gave her rest." She "had gone away," Tad later wrote, recalling feelings of "helplessness and despair, a dumb animal terror." The young mother's death, he said, left "three small children, adrift on the wreck of their little world," at the mercy of strangers.

Less than two years later, Bert found out just how coldhearted strangers can be when at an Oregon depot he first looked up into the flinty eyes of Uncle John Minthorn. After Huldah's death, relatives had parceled out the three orphans among themselves, then uprooted Bert yet again. "Thee is going to Oregon," an uncle informed him. They put the eleven-year-old on a westbound emigrant coach of the Union Pacific for a bare-bones seven-day journey across the Great Plains and the Rockies and then by river steamer on the Willamette to Newberg—his first view of the West, with which he ever after identified. Bereft of parents, catapulted toward a destination he could not imagine, he carried with him a prayer card reading, "Leave me not, neither forsake me, Oh God of my salvation."

Charles Dickens would have had no difficulty recognizing Uncle John—country doctor, Indian agent under Chester Arthur, and school official. Hard-bitten, ambitious, avaricious, he believed "idle hands were the work of the devil." He quickly determined that Bert, dispatched to take the place of his son who had died at seven, would not do. Bert returned the ill favor. For the next six years, they lived together in a sullen truce. Bert engaged in hard labor— felling trees, splitting logs, clearing stumps—six days a week, with all of each Sabbath given over to religious observance. In later years, a woman who ran a restaurant in the Oregon town commented, "I can recall him in so many different circumstances, and all of them are tinged with a bit of pathos, as if life had cheated him of his full share of youthful enjoyment."

"I do not think he was very happy," Dr. Minthorn said. "Our home was not like the one he left with his own parents in it (indulgent) and with very little responsibility and almost no work. . . . He always seemed to me to resent . . . being told to do anything." When Bert enrolled at Friends Pacific Academy (today evangelical George Fox University) in Newberg, ensconced in the superintendent's office was Uncle John—called by another nephew "the greatest disciplinarian I ever saw."

Their discord became more muted when, in 1888, Minthorn launched a new career as a real estate promoter in the state capital, Salem. Bert dropped out of school to become part-time office boy and full-time hustler. Not yet fourteen, he met prospects at the station, escorted them to boardinghouses, and then took them on tours of the Oregon Land Company's pear orchard plots in the Willamette Valley—all the while reciting Minthorn's spiels. Hardworking and a quick study, he picked up bookkeeping and typing during the day and attended business college in the evening. More than one night he slept in the office. Asked a generation later about his boyhood goal, he answered: "To be able to earn my own living without the help of anybody, anywhere." His uncle, who came to appreciate Bert's industriousness and ingenuity, put him in charge of national advertising (Lord and Thomas of Chicago ran one of their ads in a thousand papers) and of dealing with luminaries as important as the Speaker of the Oregon legislature. Still, with a rudimentary education and an unremarkable personality, Bert had no reason for great expectations.

· · ·

A chance meeting with a mining engineer, though, fired Hoover's imagination. He heard that a new university, Leland Stanford, was being founded in California, and he set his cap on going there.

His meager schooling nearly derailed that aspiration when he failed the entrance examination. The Stanford mathematics professor who administered the test was so impressed by his tenacity, however, that he admitted Bert conditionally. "A young Quaker . . . none too well prepared," the examiner reported, "but showing remarkable keenness." A Quaker himself who would one day be president of Swarthmore, he noted that the slender, square-jawed applicant "put his teeth together with great decision, and his whole face and posture showed his determination to pass the examination at any cost." He instructed Bert to arrive in California well before the university opened in order to be tutored for a second test.

In late August 1891, Bert boarded a southbound train, and some weeks later Stanford welcomed him into its pioneer class—with the stipulation that he overcome his deficiency in English. That proved to be a lifetime challenge. His grasp of spelling remained precarious, and he never developed a felicitous style. "Reading Herbert Hoover's tries at political philosophy taxes the most dedicated powers of concentration," the political scientist James David Barber later wrote. "He seemed to have a positive instinct for . . . a kind of thudding Latin threnody, like balls of glue dropped from a rooftop."

The youngest student on campus, Hoover had to get by, in the words of one writer, "on a shoestring of money and a thimbleful of preparatory education." He survived thanks to odd jobs—currying horses, becoming agent for a San Jose laundry, running a lecture and concert bureau—but at the cost of shortchanging study time. In his first semester, he flunked German and did so poorly in other courses that he earned no credit at all for the term. After repeatedly failing to satisfy an English requirement, he disposed of it only because a science professor mopped up his punctuation and grammar.

Ill-equipped for college though he was, Stanford became a haven for him. In years to come, the campus in the foothills—with its red-tiled Spanish cloisters and its aromatic eucalyptus—was the hearth to which he always yearned to return. He never ceased to believe his country was the greatest nation on earth; that Westerners, especially Californians, were the most gifted of Americans; and that finest of all were Stanford men. "Stanford," he later wrote, "is the best place in the world." On that campus he found acceptance, he found his métier, he found his future wife; he almost found himself.

After Christmas of his freshman year, Hoover had the good fortune to meet a man who was to change the trajectory of his life: John Casper Branner, chair of the department of geology and state geologist of Arkansas. Hoover, hired as his typist, made such a good impression that he earned a summer position charting outcrops in the rattlesnake-infested Ozarks. On returning to campus in the fall, Hoover, who had been largely clueless about a career, switched his major to geology. At the end of his sophomore year, he assisted Branner in creating a huge topographical relief map of Arkansas for display at the Chicago World's Fair, where it won a prize, and that summer he worked with Waldemar Lindgren of the U.S. Geological Survey in the Nevada desert and the High Sierra. He performed so well that when the USGS charts appeared, they carried the name not just of Lindgren but also of the Stanford undergraduate. His fieldwork imbued him with pride of craft. "Tomorrow we are going to make descent of the American River canyon, a thing people here say is impossible," he wrote a friend. "But they are not geologists."

While gaining this priceless experience, Hoover continued to live hand to mouth. When in the summer of his junior year a survey post he was expecting did not materialize, he was reduced to driving a team of horses from Palo Alto to Yosemite, painting signs, and posting advertisements for William Randolph Hearst's *San Francisco Examiner*. On learning that he did have a job after all—in the mountains near Lake Tahoe—Hoover, all but penniless, walked more than eighty miles in three days to catch a boat in Stockton. No one could doubt his fortitude, however they may have regarded his forbidding personality.

At first, Hoover's fellow students thought him beyond reach. They saw him trudging across the quad slightly hunched over, as though to apologize for his presence, his eyes staring fixedly at the ground. He looked younger than his years but seemed prematurely old—taciturn, unsmiling. He would not speak unless spoken to, and then, avoiding eye contact, was as likely to snort as to expel a few words, while nervously rattling keys in a trouser pocket. The wife of a professor remembered him as "always blunt, almost to the point of utter tactlessness." At gatherings in her home, he "usually sat back in the corner and listened. He rarely spoke and always seemed to be a little ill at ease."

Yet, against all odds, Hoover succeeded in becoming something of a big man on campus, largely by leaguing with other outsiders against the snobbish Greek-letter societies for which he developed an abiding hatred. (In later years, he would forbid his sons to join any Stanford fraternity.) Asked to run for class treasurer on an anti-frat slate, Hoover agreed on condition that, if elected, he would not be paid. He campaigned vigorously, and the "barbarian" ticket won. As treasurer, he put to good use the bookkeeping skills he had learned in Oregon. He also drafted a student constitution that was still in effect a half century later. Too ungainly to play shortstop, he became the baseball team's financial manager and served the same function for the football squad, even arranging one of the first "Big Games" in the school's storied rivalry with the University of California. " 'Popularity' is not exactly the word for his . . . influence on his fellows," his future biographer Will Irwin reflected. "A better word, probably, would be 'standing.' The bleachers never rose and cheered when he passed; but subtly he . . . radiated leadership." By the end of his four years, Hoover had collected a number of life-long buddies who would one day count themselves loyal followers of the Stanford alum they were to designate "the Chief."

He had acquired one particular friend. Geology was demarcated as male turf, but in his senior year a spirited young woman with a beguiling smile enrolled as a freshman in the program. In conversations in the lab and in the field, Hoover learned that Lou Henry not only shared his love of the outdoors, but also that, though her home was in Monterey, she was Iowa-born. By November he was reporting, "We have a young lady taking Geology as a specialty now a very nice young lady too." Hoover was smitten, but there was no way that he could propose. On graduating from Stanford in 1895, he had but forty dollars to his name. The only work he could find—in the depths of the worst depression of the nineteenth century—was pushing a handcar through dank tunnels in the bowels of a gold mine, ten hours a night, seven days a week. Even that menial job in Bret Harte country petered out, and, save for a brief stint with Cornish migrants in the Nevada City pits, Hoover spent the rest of the year, as he later wrote, in "ceaseless tramping and ceaseless refusal." Long afterward, he recalled, "I then learned what the bottom levels of real human despair are paved with." In such circumstances, the most that Bert could venture with Lou was an "understanding."

Early in 1896 in San Francisco, his fortunes took a decided turn for the better when he knocked on the door of Louis Janin, a prominent mining engineer who was an agent for the Rothschilds. Janin took him on as a copyist, little more than an office boy, but soon found Hoover's know-how valuable in litigation and in assessing New Mexico and Colorado mines. When the world-renowned London firm of Bewick, Moreing and Company told Janin it was seeking an engineer (at least thirty-five years old) with expertise in smelting to go to Australia as a mine scout, he recommended Hoover. Much too young—only twenty-two—the recent graduate grew a mustache, bought a top hat and a frock coat, puffed up his credentials, crossed the country by rail, and sailed out of New York harbor on a White Star liner for the Old World. On his country estate in England, Charles Algernon Moreing looked Hoover over, liked what he saw, and sent the young recruit (who gave his age as thirty-six) by train through the Alps to the ancient Roman port of Brindisi, then on a long voyage via the Suez Canal and the Indian Ocean, with stops at Port Said and Ceylon, to the land down under. For the first time in his life, Hoover later said, "history became a reality and America a contrast."

· · ·

Not in his worst nightmare could Hoover have conjured up what awaited him. Australia, he wrote home, was "a country of red dust, black flies, and white heat," and Coolgardie—called a town of "sin, sand, sorrow, sickness, and sore eyes"—a hellhole. In Kalgoorlie, his next location, the thermometer at night often did not drop below 100°, and typhoid fever claimed three men a day. Mine inspection trips to spots as remote as Never Never in a land of dwarf kangaroos required exhausting journeys on blindfolded Afghan camels across trackless wastelands—in the phrase of one of his early biographers, "an insanity of monotony."

Yet Hoover thrived. Bewick, Moreing started him off with a handsome salary and a cottage with a cook. He also had a valet. But Hoover spent little time at his comfortable home. Over the next eighteen months, he logged more than five thousand miles in the bush, probing strata for veins of gold. His great coup was the Sons of Gwalia mine. In later years, Hoover, who habitually overstated his achievements, assigned himself more credit than merited for discovering this fabulous lode—which, as its name conveys, was first worked by Welshmen. But he did, after assaying the site, advise the company to purchase it. From an initial investment of little more than a million dollars, Bewick, Moreing eventually raked in $65 million. To manage the Sons of Gwalia and seven other mines, Moreing chose Hoover—with a boost in salary and responsibility for scores of employees.

He was a tough boss. A mere stripling, Hoover had no qualms about firing eight men from his staff while confiding to a friend back home that a number of others were "in the noose." He was "dreadfully put out," he said, by resolving to discharge a seventy-two-year-old accountant, "but I have to get things in shape for the company." In the fall of 1897, he extended the workweek from forty-four to forty-eight hours, and the following spring he reported to the London office:

> The Truckers in the lower level struck for a rise in pay owing to the wet ground. We discharged the entire crew at that level and replaced them with men at the old rate.
>
> Again it had been formerly the custom to pay double pay for Sunday Work, which we stopped, and six men working

on Sunday refused to proceed. We discharged them and replaced them with new men.

I have a bunch of Italians coming up this week and will put them in the mine on contract work. If they are satisfactory I will secure enough of them to hold the property in case of a general strike, and with your permission will reduce wages.

In his *Memoirs* a half century later, he wrote of "the sheer joy" not only "of creating productive enterprises," but also "of correcting the perversities and incompetence of men."

In fact, Hoover held far less liberal social views than contemporary tories. He opposed Australia's workmen's compensation act as too "prejudicial to the owners"; deplored the imposition of a minimum wage; objected to closing ore treatment mills on Sundays; and advocated a "system" to blacklist "the demagogue." Bewick, Moreing, which imported Italian laborers because they were more tractable, thrived by getting rid of large numbers of employees. Whenever Hoover appeared on the scene, workers wondered how many of them had seen their last payday.

Hoover's frigid demeanor and his Yankee brag earned him as much animosity as his hard-nosed procedures. Many found him abrasive, abrupt, and overbearing as well as solitary. When you were with Hoover, commented one who knew him well, you were always conscious of "a certain atmosphere of aggressiveness." A journalist observed that the only subject Hoover took any pleasure in discussing—in a "dull, toneless voice"—was work, "if his harsh staccato 'yep' and 'nope' could be elevated to the level of discussion." When Hoover did speak, a Melbourne reporter noted (as had his fellow students at Stanford), he averted his eyes. He was without humor and, so far as anyone could tell, without emotion. He had few, if any, friends who were equals—then, and for the rest of his days. Hoover, Arthur Schlesinger Jr. later wrote, lived a life that seemed to come out of the pages of the globe-trotting war correspondent Richard Harding Davis, but "he transmuted all adventure into business, as a Davis hero would transmute all business into adventure."

In the course of a lifetime, few Americans spent more years abroad than Hoover, but, wherever he lived, he came—sooner or later, and mostly sooner—to lament that his host nation did not measure up to the United States. "No country in the world," he said of western Australia, "has witnessed such rank swindling and charlatan engineering." The Aussies and the Brits down under, he found, did not like him any more than he liked them. With characteristic indifference to punctuation, Hoover complained: "They only have us because they have to they don't know how to make their mines pay dividends we do." In London, years later, he would celebrate not only the Fourth of July but the anniversary of California's admission to the Union. (Hoover's romance with California, an acquaintance remarked, brought to mind Virgil's reveries about Italy.) His first initials, "H.C.," critics said, stood for "Hail Columbia."

The young man's employers, though, knew that they had lucked into a wunderkind. They did not at all mind being represented by an agent whose talisman was "efficiency" and who sought to give the firm an edge over its competitors by extracting, in his words, more "work per man per day." To boot, he was a whiz at assessing the potential of mines. After the Sons of Gwalia acquisition, Bewick, Moreing promoted him to junior partner with a share in profits that would net him ten thousand dollars a year (many times that sum today), and in the fall of 1898 the firm offered him a lucrative opportunity to supervise a vast new engineering operation in China.

His future secured, Hoover cabled Lou Henry, "Will you marry me?" Almost as soon as she cabled back her speedy acceptance, he set sail from Perth for London to discuss China investments with Algernon Moreing, then crossed the Atlantic and the United States for a reunion with Lou in Monterey. There they were wed in the bride's family parlor. Less than a fortnight later, outfitted with dozens of books on China, they embarked for the Far East. Hoover had circumnavigated the globe, a transit he would make—by sea and by land—four more times in the next decade.

. . .

China gave the newlyweds greater adventure than they had bargained for. In 1900 they found themselves besieged in the international settlement at Tientsin by a rabidly xenophobic order. The Boxers—three hundred thousand strong—massacred Chinese Christians, torched churches, murdered the German envoy, and vowed to drive "the foreign devils" into the sea. Hoover erected barricades of grain and sugar sacks and organized distribution of rice and water to pro-Western Chinese sheltered in their compound. Meanwhile, Lou—a .38 Mauser pistol tucked under her belt—bicycled about on errands under fire (five shells hit the Hoover home), nursed the wounded, tended a dairy herd, and kept night vigils. After a harrowing twenty-eight days, the siege was broken. "I do not remember a more satisfying musical performance," Hoover later said, "than the bugles of the American Marines entering the settlement playing 'There'll Be a Hot Time in the Old Town Tonight.' "

The Marine Corps band could well have struck up "Yankee Doodle" to orchestrate Hoover's imperial mind-set. "Unless our Government adopts a most forcible policy, we will have a calamity in China that has not been equaled in the history of the world," he asserted. "Diplomacy with an Asiatic is of no use. If you are going to do business with him you must begin your talk with a gun in your hand, and let him know that you will use it." His experience in the Australian mines had led him to the conclusion that "Asiatics and negroes" were of a "low mental order" and that "one white man equals from two to three of the colored races, even in the simplest forms of mine work such as shoveling." Placed in charge of a workforce in the Chinese Engineering Company—the biggest firm in the Celestial Empire—he alluded to his laborers as "9000 thieves," and, after an inspection trip, recommended "a thorough sweeping of useless employees." Still worse, he thought, were "the unspeakable villainy of Chinese administration" and "the rottenness of Chinese officialdom."

It was asking too much to imagine that Hoover would relate easily to a manager who indulged in opium, but, though he traveled widely—beyond the Gobi Desert to Outer Mongolia, where he met the "Living Buddha"—Hoover did not adapt at all. In Tientsin, he rented a commodious house on the outskirts of the foreign settlement that removed him from the local populace, save for his fifteen Chinese servants. "A scholar, a diplomat, or a missionary who has lived in the Orient might be expected to acquire . . . some sensibility toward another culture," his biographer David Burner has observed. "What the East taught Hoover, however, was almost the opposite. He learned to think of Western technology . . . as offering a means of reordering whole societies." Traditional communities, in turn, did not take well to an obsessive modernizer. A Kaiping associate complained that the American came up with "all sorts of schemes" that "did not conform to Chinese usages."

Hoover magnified his difficulties in collaboration by assuming an ambiguous role. After foreign armies began to seize the assets of the Chinese Engineering Company, he arranged to convert the firm into a British limited liability corporation, a transfer that put him in the peculiar position of working both for the Chinese government and for Bewick, Moreing—a relationship guaranteed to beget grievances. Exactly one month after pledging that a China board would have "the entire management," he urged C. Algernon Moreing to move the head office out of Tientsin to prevent "any interference from the 'China Board.'" Hoover and a Belgian partner later acknowledged that they had limited "Chinese intervention" to a "harmless" consultative body in order to lodge control "in foreign hands." (When he ran for president in 1928, he would be accused of having been an unscrupulous double agent.) For his services, Hoover pocketed around $200,000 (more than $4 million today). The 1901 acquisition of the Kaiping mines, which has been ranked as "the largest transfer of property to foreigners in the history of

China," precipitated a lawsuit of such magnitude that it was closely followed even by King Edward VII.

It is unlikely that the precise nature of Hoover's activities in China will ever be sorted out. Hoover believed that the Chinese with whom he was dealing were corrupt and incompetent, and he was quite possibly right. The Chinese thought Hoover was a swindler, and he was certainly capable of sharp dealing. In Australia, he had advocated lying about monthly output in order to mislead investors. British Foreign Office representatives concluded that the dispute between the Westerners, including the Moreing group, and the Chinese was "a case of rogues falling out" after behavior that was "very shady on both sides," and the British chargé at Peking had "small doubt that Messrs. Moreing and others have made a pretty pile at the expense of the Chinese." However questionable some of his actions may have been, Hoover proved invaluable to his employers. By skillful administration and an infusion of capital, he turned the immense Kaiping coal deposits into a flourishing enterprise. He was duly rewarded.

In the autumn of 1901, Hoover departed China for London, where he was to become, at twenty-seven, one of four partners of Bewick, Moreing, called "perhaps the most noted mining syndicate in the world." After an interview in California—a stop on his long journey from Asia across the Pacific to America and then, after a transcontinental rail trip, across the Atlantic to Europe—the *San Francisco Chronicle* wrote that Hoover was "reputed to be the highest salaried man of his years in the world."

The Hoovers took up residence in London, first at 39 Hyde Park Gate, then in Campden Hill. Their Kensington villa boasted French windows, a walnut-paneled dining room, and an oak-paneled library. In the walled garden of the Red House, callers came upon a fish pond, a towering mulberry tree, and a fountain. The retinue of servants included a butler, a chauffeur, a cook, a parlor maid, and a governess. On occasion, this congenial abode allowed Hoover to show a side of himself that those beyond the family hearth rarely saw. At Easter he hid colored eggs in the garden, and at Christmas he dressed up as Santa and distributed presents to servants and their children.

Instead of easing into this appealing urban retreat and an office chair in the City, Hoover roamed the world on behalf of Bewick, Moreing over the next seven years. In 1907 he sailed for Australia, leaving behind in London his pregnant wife and three-year-old son. They were not to lay eyes on him again for six months. Having learned nothing from his own painful childhood, he turned his two boys over to others through most of their early and teenage years. When illnesses laid them low, neither father nor mother was at their bedside.

His peregrinations as a mine evaluator caught him up in happenings of a sort that are staples of novels set in exotic locales—or of penny dreadfuls. In Asia, as Richard Norton Smith has written, Hoover "saw the world of Kipling and Maugham." To check out mining property in Korea, he rode that fabled thoroughfare of intrigue the Trans-Siberian Railway. One day in Burma, while crawling through a mine, he came upon unfamiliar prints in the mud, then backed out hastily when he realized that they were the fresh tracks of a Bengal tiger. In Burma, too, in a delirium from malaria, Hoover was overcome by a desire to write poetry.

In these years and later, he carried on reconnaissances in Australia. His eye was not always unerring. He rated East Murchison United "the big mine of the north" with "a splendid career before it," but investors lost their shirts before the operation was liquidated, and a risky flier at Loddon Valley, after devouring several million dollars, wound up, in the words of its chairman, a "ghastly failure." Nevertheless, a man knowledgeable about the Australian gold fields said of Hoover that there was "no cleverer engineer in the two hemispheres."

• • •

In 1908 Hoover reached a major decision—to go into business on his own. He sold his interest in Bewick, Moreing, he explained a few years after, "for about $225,000 cash as I could not stand

Moreing any longer than necessary having given practically 5 years to that mess." That explanation was less than frank. It was true he found C. Algernon Moreing "wholly impossible." Moreing, for his part, wound up suing Hoover after a nasty spat. But there were more compelling reasons for the rupture. One was that Hoover had worked himself into a breakdown, or something close. (In 1904, plagued by insomnia, his memory erratic, he had been ordered by his physician to take a two-month voyage to South Africa— without wife or infant son—to see if he could pull himself together.) The other was that he was determined to get rich. Most folks would have thought he had already accumulated a tidy sum— several hundred thousand dollars at a time of no income tax. But for Hoover that was not enough. "If a man has not made a million dollars by the time he is forty," he said, "he is not worth much." And, by his lights, he was getting on in years. He was thirty-three.

With offices at Number 1 London Wall and in New York, San Francisco, Paris, Petrograd, and Mandalay, Hoover ran his own consulting firm in a style that a later generation would term "multinational." As "the doctor of sick mines," he specialized in reviving ailing enterprises in return for a share of the profits. Though he insisted on being regarded as an engineer, he was actually more a financier and promoter who, in addition to serving as technical consultant, participated in pools to manipulate the stock market. He did not admire all businessmen—some were "drones"—but he sang the praises of "insiders" like himself while denigrating small-fry investors not in the know as "idiots."

Hoover's operations ranged from the Klondike to Tierra del Fuego, from tin diggings in Cornwall to a copper smelter in the Urals. As Schlesinger wrote, Hoover "traveled endlessly, from Mandalay to the Transvaal, from Egypt to the Malay States, from a turquoise mine at Mount Sinai to the foggy, gas-lit streets of the City of London." He owned shares in the Brazilian Iron Syndicate, Russo-Asiatic Consolidated, and the Inter-Argentine Syndicate, and he reorganized oil explorations in Peru and Trinidad. His most unpromising venture—in the forbidding terrain of Burma—would eventually become the main source of his income. For eight years, he persevered against obstacles that would have cowed another man, and in 1913 his doggedness paid off when workers penetrated a fabulous lode of silver, zinc, and lead. Hoover later wrote of this "great enterprise" that he "took it as bare jungle and left it with 25,000 men employed and a new town on earth." True, some of his investments, always undertaken with supreme confidence, were flops. But others were, after numerous mishaps, extraordinary successes— notably the creation in Australia of the awesome Zinc Corporation. "In the domain of practical mining finance," a leading periodical in the field said of Hoover, "no one holds a more assured position."

High regard did not always imply affection, for wherever Hoover went—Australia, China, England—he feuded, repeatedly clashing with associates and not infrequently striving to get them fired. Though he had a brilliant career, he also revealed a troublesome tendency toward self-delusion. When something went wrong, he would either blame others or claim that the failure demonstrated his foresight. Self-righteous, he bridled at even mild criticism. "Despite his persona of disinterested objectivity and his reputation as a cool, aloof businessman, Hoover in some ways was like a volcano: hot and smoldering underneath," George H. Nash has written in his superb account of these years. At one point, Hoover said unapologetically, "I have insisted on having my own way." If he could not do so, he flew into rages.

Spasmodically during this period, Hoover talked of abandoning profit seeking for "some job of public service . . . in government and all that sort of thing." As early as 1907, he confided that "he had run through his profession" and "just making money wasn't enough." Moreover, he doubted that there would be any more mining bonanzas. What would he like to do? "Get into the big game somewhere," Hoover responded. But year after year went by, and he did not break away. Something drove him from continent to continent, from one prospect to the next. When he did begin a new life, he later said, it would be "at home, of course." Through all of 1907 and 1908, and again in 1910, though, he did not spend a single day in America.

Hoover's identity as a technician allayed his uneasiness about chasing dollars rather than performing "public service." Out of his seasoning in Australia and perhaps his exposure to the theories of the sociologist Thorstein Veblen, who had joined the Stanford faculty, Hoover began to recast his social outlook. Like the author of *The Theory of the Leisure Class* and *The Instinct of Workmanship and the State of the Industrial Arts*, he esteemed engineers as "the real brains of industrial progress"—disinterested, altruistic craftsmen who were the hope of the future. "Engineering without imagination sinks to a trade," he said. At a time of tremendous growth—the total of 7,000 engineers in the America of Hoover's youth in 1880 rose to 226,000 by 1930—Hoover claimed for them professional status, and more. In contrast to occupations that were "parasitic," engineers with a sense of mission could, through their diligence and precision, transmute "a figment of the imagination" into a project that "brings jobs and homes to men," which "then . . . elevates the standards of living and adds to the comforts of life." He shared the outlook of the president of an engineering society who asserted, "The golden rule will be put into practice by the slide rule of the engineer."

Hoover pulled together lectures he had given at the Columbia School of Mines and at Stanford into a volume titled *Principles of Mining*, published in 1909. It was not elegant. The publisher said of his manuscript: "It was atrociously bad—bad in handwriting, in spelling, in grammar and syntax, and in composition." Much of it had to be rewritten. Indifferent to its literary shortcomings, Hoover concentrated on conveying the substance of what he had learned about how to succeed in the industry. For years afterward, mine schools embraced *Principles* as a basic text. Some passages in the book, which mostly dealt with matters such as valuation, revealed that Hoover was developing a more progressive attitude toward labor than in his first years in Australia. He favored not only high wages (in return for hard work), but also the eight-hour workday and improved mine safety. He accepted organized labor—less out of sympathy with workers than because unions that acceded "the rights of their employers" could maintain control over their members and would spare management "the constant harassment of possible strikes." Still, he thought unions "normal and proper antidotes for unlimited capitalistic organization" and declared, "The time when the employer could ride roughshod over his labor is disappearing with the doctrine of 'laissez-faire' on which it is founded."

Intellectual curiosity and a desire to enhance the prestige of the engineering profession led Hoover to collaborate with his wife in preparing an English edition of *De Re Metallica*, a 1556 treatise on mining and metallurgy by a German who adopted the pen name of Agricola. The idea originated with Lou, who had a command of Latin. To carry it out, Hoover spent twenty thousand dollars employing a team of research assistants and translators able to cope with medieval German and faux Latin. Hoover's extensive annotation of the manual furnished a history of mining from ancient times and elucidated technical terms. His commentary on labor conditions gave further evidence of his increasingly enlightened views in a year when he contributed a thousand dollars to Teddy Roosevelt's Bull Moose campaign. Published in 1912, the 632-page volume, bound in vellum, was embellished with splendid reproductions of the original woodcuts.

• • •

In 1912 Hoover's gossamer fancies about a new start in life began to become more credible. "I have got to that stage now where I am playing the game for the game's sake, as the counters don't interest me any longer," he said. A millionaire four times over, he had more than reached his goal. In addition, having been away from his homeland almost constantly since 1897, he was morose. "The American is always an alien abroad," he wrote home. "He never can assimilate, nor do other peoples ever accept him otherwise than a foreigner." With no insight about how his own deportment might affect others, he added, "I am disgusted with myself when I think how much better off you people are who stuck by your own country and place. When you walk down the street you meet a hundred men who have a genuine pleasure in greeting you. I am an alien who gets a grin once in nine months."

Londoners, in truth, did not find "star-spangled Hoover" captivating or endearing. A British compeer remembered that "he was a very hardworking, hardheaded and rather saturnine man, and always struck me as a little uncouth." Impersonating British aristocrats, Bert and Lou Hoover—far distanced from their Iowa roots—dressed for dinner each night, but they were parvenus. Sunday evenings at Red House could be tedious. Hoover himself acknowledged that at parties he "felt like a wet crow." He "had no small talk—no small talk whatever," an acquaintance commented, and he refused to make the minimal effort expected of a host. A woman who tried to converse with Hoover found him "not a very affable dinner partner." He was, she said, "a grunter. I would say something and he'd just say 'unh.'"

Hoover's reclusiveness prevented his host country from perceiving that the American was not always as self-centered and unfeeling as he seemed. Hoover saw to it that each month a sizable chunk of his salary went to needy friends and relatives in the United States. The recipients of his largesse did not know it came from Hoover, who pursued what one friend called "good deeds by stealth," so as not to draw attention to himself. He was especially solicitous of young men trying to make it on their own as he had. He told his secret emissary to make sure that "boys who are still in the struggle stages will not hesitate to draw on my account to its utmost limits." Sometimes his benefactions took more tangible forms, as when a Stanford professor acquired a rare book that he could not afford to purchase. Not until long after did Ray Lyman Wilbur, later president of Stanford and a member of Hoover's cabinet, learn the source of a gift that had made his subsequent success possible.

Attachment to Stanford allowed Hoover to ease into community service when toward the end of 1912 he accepted election as a trustee of the university, a post he would hold for nearly half a century. He took on this responsibility with characteristic gusto. In ten days, the head of the board of trustees observed, Hoover came up with more ideas than they had heard in ten years. Hoover pushed through a program to build not only a new library, but also a hospital and a gymnasium. Conceiving of a student union as a haven that would "inoculate against the bacillus of social inequality" and avoid "the undemocratic social stratification which has been so much discussed of late in our eastern neighbors," he quietly donated $100,000 toward its construction. "It is marvelous," the university president confided, "how Hoover is handling our Board. Almost every reform we have dreamed of has slipped through as if oiled."

The new trustee had more in mind. He was distressed to learn that assistant professors could not afford domestic servants and that their wives needed to perform housework. Never one to shirk detail, he set down next to the name of each of the 160 or so members of the faculty the precise amount of salary raise he thought each deserved, and, astonishingly, the board approved his figures unchanged. That phenomenal expression of faith in one man's judgment did not begin to satisfy Hoover. He was looking for a still larger stage in the public sphere.

Opportunity for more conspicuous service came when he agreed to be overseas agent for the Panama-Pacific International Exposition set for 1915 to celebrate the anniversary of Balboa's discovery of the vast western sea. His goal was extraordinarily ambitious—nothing less than to coax King George V to leave St. James's Palace and sail all the way to San Francisco via the Panama Canal to give royal imprimatur to the California exhibition. Well connected in British political and publishing purlieus, Hoover conferred with the former prime minister Arthur Balfour and won the publishing potentate Lord Northcliffe to his side. In later years, never willing to acknowledge failure, he implied that he had persuaded England and Germany to participate when, in fact, both turned him down. His effort, though, did have one life-changing upshot. It placed him in London in 1914 when the booming guns of August heralded the outbreak of world war.

2

The Great Humanitarian

On August 6, 1914, two days after Germany invaded neutral Belgium and four days before his fortieth birthday, Hoover took up a command post at London's Savoy Hotel ballroom in the midst of a milling throng of panicky Americans. More than one hundred thousand U.S. nationals were fleeing the Continent only to find that their letters of credit could not be cashed and there was no way to buy passage home. That day Hoover had organized a group of U.S. businessmen in the City into a "Committee of American Residents in London for Assistance of American Travellers." He had been dragooned into the task, he claimed. In fact, he had been pushy. In wresting control of the operation from another group, Hoover maintained that he had the sponsorship of the U.S. ambassador, Walter Hines Page—who had no knowledge of what Hoover was doing.

Brazen though he was, Hoover, displaying superb managerial skills, deserved all the plaudits he was to receive. Even before the event at the Savoy, he had pulled together every shilling and tuppence he could lay hands on and had doled out small loans to his stranded countrymen. Each day brought legions of arrivals, and his committee sustained them—men, women, and children—until they could book passage to the United States, then advanced money for tickets in steerage. In these days of acute anxiety,

Hoover was unflappable. When one matron angrily insisted upon a written guarantee that no U-boat would sink her ship on the transatlantic voyage, he coolly wrote her out a pledge. Over the course of two months in which Hoover worked indefatigably, the group raised and disbursed some $400,000. Almost every dollar was repaid.

To Hoover, the experience offered the first of a series of proofs he took to heart: voluntarism and private charity could answer any crisis; it was not necessary to involve the state. He gave little notice to the reality that he had been able to act with such authority because his committee had been granted semiofficial status. Nor did he heed that the sizable sum of $150,000 he distributed had come from the U.S. government.

His task completed, Hoover packed his bags to sail home on the RMS *Lusitania* in mid-October, only to receive an urgent summons from the U.S. embassy. The situation in Belgium, Ambassador Page told him, had become desperate. German armies had uprooted more than a million Belgians, ruthlessly wiped out hundreds of villages, destroyed factories, demolished means of transportation, and seized crops and livestock. In addition, the British, to starve the Reich into submission, had imposed a blockade on the whole continent, closing off shipments to a country that imported 70 percent of its food. The Belgians faced mass starvation within two weeks. Brussels had only a four-day stock of flour. Would Hoover agree to head a private undertaking (with the unofficial sanction of the U.S. government) to save the Belgians from famine?

As chairman of the Commission for Relief in Belgium, Hoover took on a daunting mission. He needed to raise a million dollars a week; buy tens of thousands of tons of food from all quarters of the globe; see that specially marked ships took the precious cargo through perilous seas to Holland, then through canals into Belgium; and make sure that it reached the people for whom it was intended and nobody else. He did not let a moment lapse. Reckoning that the Chicago wheat exchange would be open for another hour, as soon as he returned from his meeting with Page he wired an order, and on November 4, 1914, a ship laden with food embarked for Rotterdam. Boldly, Hoover placed orders for foodstuffs costing five times as much as the cash he had on hand and, to guarantee delivery, pledged every penny he had in the world—and more. If a man without Hoover's daring had held his post, many thousands would have starved to death.

An organization with no legal standing and no stable source of funds, the Commission for Relief in Belgium crossed national frontiers in the midst of the world's first global war, plunged into markets on two continents, and spent unheard-of sums. Nothing daunted Hoover. He seized control of railways, took over factories and warehouses, and commandeered five hundred Belgian canal boats. When the kaiser's armies occupied northern France, Hoover extended his realm there too. The CRB, said a British Foreign Office functionary, was "a piratical state organized for benevolence."

Provisioning the Belgians required Hoover to engage in delicate transactions with the belligerents. Early in 1915, he conferred with Chancellor of the Exchequer David Lloyd George and Reich Chancellor Theobald von Bethmann Hollweg. To enlist greater support from the French, he met with the president of the Third Republic, Raymond Poincaré. Ambassador Page said of Hoover: "He is probably the only man living who has privately (i.e. without holding office) negotiated understandings with the British, French, German, Dutch and Belgian Gov'ts." So unorthodox was this behavior that Senator Henry Cabot Lodge threatened to prosecute Hoover under the Logan Act of 1799, which prohibited U.S. citizens from engaging in diplomatic dealings with foreign powers, until the senator's good friend Teddy Roosevelt quieted him. "I will hold his hand," T.R. assured Hoover.

Though well before the war Hoover had established a close relationship with a number of government leaders in England, especially Sir Edward Grey, the Germans unexpectedly proved more tractable than the British. Hoover secured from the Reich a passport reading "This man is not to be stopped anywhere under any circumstances," and when General von Bissing, the imperious governor-general of Belgium, became confrontational, Hoover hastened to Berlin and had him overruled. The British, reasonably enough, asked why they should allow their blockade to be perforated. Incensed at his lack of sympathy, the First Lord of the Admiralty, Winston Churchill, called Hoover an SOB.

Churchill was not the only one to curse out Hoover or to find him obnoxious. "Tact," Lloyd George remarked, "is not one of his many qualities." Hoover, he later said, "had a surliness of mien and a peremptoriness of speech." Similarly, the Belgian minister in London found Hoover's style of speaking *"parfois impératif."* He was chronically bad tempered—quick to take offense, primed to scent conspirators leagued against him, unwilling to control outbursts of rage. Again and again, as in meetings with Spanish diplomats, he blew a fuse. Even someone who thought well of Hoover remarked, "He can express himself so accurately and so indignantly that his victim will go off nursing a grudge for the rest of his natural life."

The U.S. ambassador to Belgium, Brand Whitlock, who had won renown as reform mayor of Toledo, Ohio, started out with great goodwill toward Hoover but wound up loathing him. In the early days of the CRB, Whitlock wrote that Hoover "has a genius for organization and for getting things done, and beneath all, with his great intelligence, . . . has a wonderful human heart." It did not take long, though, for the envoy to conclude that Hoover was *"fruste"* (uncultivated) and "boorish," or to deplore his acting "in a brutal manner." After reading a domineering cable to the king of the Belgians drafted by the CRB chairman, Whitlock commented that Hoover was "always trying to force, to blackmail, to frighten people into doing things his way. . . . What a bully! He would even bully a poor exiled King!"

. . .

Throughout his tenure, Hoover insisted on deference to his will. He had hardly begun work when he announced that "it has got to be recognized by everybody . . . that I am the boss, and that any attempts to minimize the importance of my leadership would do . . . infinite harm." Hoover "did not like you to disagree with him," one of his subordinates later commented. "He *definitely* did not like you to disagree with him." In his relations with foreign leaders, he repeatedly threatened to take his marbles and go home if he was not given his way. "After many sleepless nights, I went to Belgium and found everybody dead against me," he told a friend. "I stayed there a little over two weeks. . . . I . . . brought Whitlock to my side within twenty minutes—I had the Belgians my way in 24 hours and in a week the Americans in control were either bashed into line or were eating out of my hand." Subsequently, he confided by cable, "We will train a machine gun on our troublesome friends this week."

Many who had dealings with Hoover found him soul chilling. He was capable of traveling all the way to Belgium without uttering a word to the men accompanying him. He avoided personal encounters with the starving—even with children, though he was known to be concerned about their welfare. Hoover had become, the historian Kendrick Clements has commented perceptively, "very much like those relatives who had taken in the young orphan," people who "sustained his body but offered . . . little emotional support." When at the end of his London stay in April 1917, a large group of colleagues turned out at Euston station to bid him farewell, he buried his head in correspondence at a window seat and never waved back or even looked up. After he arrived in Washington that spring, Secretary of the Navy Josephus Daniels, who had been eager to meet the Great Humanitarian, reported, "He told of the big work in Belgium as coldly as if he were giving statistics of production. From his words and his manner he seemed to regard human beings as so many numbers. Not once did he show the slightest feeling."

Some of his detachment may be attributed to the burdens he bore. Later, Lou Hoover wrote their children: "Those years of his life, and ours, he gave up to the cause of the little man. . . . And not only those *years*, but most of the kind of happiness, of pleasure, that had been his before. A certain . . . kind of joy was stamped out of him by those war years. Can you remember that . . . he completely changed? Not that he became altogether solemn . . . , but the old sparkling spontaneity is now only occasionally glimpsed far below the surface." The letter only hints at the price his family paid. When in 1915 Lou left England for a five-month stay in California, her husband did not see her off; instead, he sent a three-word telegram to the Liverpool dock. And there were stretches when the boys had neither mother nor father with them.

Yet, however icy Hoover was, no one questioned that he was prodigiously effective. Lord Eustace Percy in the British Foreign Office regarded the American as "the bluntest man in Europe," but acknowledged that he was "able, without apparent effort, to handle a situation involving more irreconcilable elements than any other situation in this war." On one occasion, a high-placed British official told him, "Men have gone to the Tower for less than you have done," but then acceded to demands that shortly before he had said were "out of the question."

Moreover, Hoover had some redeeming qualities that were not readily discernible. Though often greedy as an engineer and administrator to claim credit not due him, he went out of his way to make sure that his name was not publicly associated with charitable deeds—perhaps because of an ingrained Quaker sense that promoting oneself was unworthy. He also was generous toward subordinates. In 1915 Hoover told Ray Lyman Wilbur: "There is one bit of advice that I will hazard you . . . and that is never to be afraid of the ability of one's lieutenants but to bear in mind that the more able the men with whom one surrounds oneself the more certainty one has of ultimate success." That year, one of the young men under him wrote, "Mr. Hoover is such a fine, quiet, kindly man that everybody votes for him on sight—and no second choice! . . . If you want to start a wave of enthusiasm among the younger members of the C.R.B., simply say 'Mr. Hoover.' . . . He has no idea of our absolute loyalty." He added on another occasion, "Though he never notices any of us very much we all idolize him."

Much of his staff's devotion doubtless derived from recognition that Hoover spared himself no ordeal. In October 1914 he made his first inspection of war-ravaged Belgium. Before he could embark, British intelligence forced him to undergo a humiliating strip to the buff, and on landfall, the Germans required him to bare himself again. The Channel crossing held far worse perils, but Hoover repeatedly set out over the mine-strewn waters, never knowing if he would reach the farther shore. In January 1915 Ambassador Page wrote President Wilson: "Life is worth more, too, for knowing Hoover. But for him Belgium would now be starved. . . . He's a simple, modest energetic little man who began his career in California and will end it in Heaven, and he doesn't want anybody's thanks."

His skill and daring as an administrator astonished friend and foe. He operated on a colossal scale. When, after returning to America, he was pressed by an inquisitorial Oklahoma senator to state the price of a bushel of beans, Hoover retorted, "I have always bought them by the ton." An audacious manipulator, he exasperated agents of the Allies and of the Central Powers by deception and casuistry. Sometimes he told outright lies. In a period when he knew that the Germans were stealing food intended for the Belgians, he assured the British that his delivery system was impregnable. But as a British editor said, Hoover "won admiration from most and extorted respect from all." The Belgian minister to Great Britain marveled at Hoover's *"rapidité de décision"* and his capacity to create *"cet extraordinaire mécanisme."* An inspector for the Rockefeller Foundation who had closely scrutinized his operation was even more laudatory. "Mr. Hoover," concluded the future U.S. senator Frederic C. Walcott, "is a perfect wonder."

"By the end of 1916," George Nash has written, Hoover "stood preeminent in the greatest humanitarian undertaking the world had ever seen." He had raised and spent millions of dollars, with trifling overhead and not a penny lost to fraud. At its peak, his organization was feeding nine million Belgians and French a day. Hoover took special pains to care for Belgium's world-famous lacemakers. In addition to feeding the forty thousand women, he saw to it that they were supplied with thread so that they could carry on their precious craft. Under a "*soupe scolaire*" program, some two million children got a hot lunch of filling vegetable soup with white bread, and, thanks to Hoover, cocoa too.

Hoover drew from this experience the same lesson he believed he had learned in aiding the Americans stranded in London in 1914—that one should rely not on government but on civic-minded individuals "imbued with the spirit of self-sacrifice in full measure." He had been able to recruit a staff of 350 volunteers, including more than two dozen Rhodes scholars domiciled in England and "gentlemen of wide commercial experience . . . willing to devote their entire time, at their own expense." In the course of the war, his aversion to the state rigidified. Semaphoring the attitude he would take during the Great Depression, Hoover called a plan to aid Belgians rendered jobless by the German invasion "socially wrongly founded." He told Belgium's finance minister, "I cannot see anything but social harm in giving workmen payment as a right for idleness."

His celebration of voluntarism badly distorted the historical record. Even at the start, Hoover had bluntly told Ambassador Page that private contributions, "no matter how great," would be of such "uncertain quantity" that it was "absolutely necessary" for the Allied governments to bankroll the venture liberally. Early in November 1914, he had notified Allied ambassadors that "Government subvention" was essential, and, less than three weeks later, he had instructed Lord Percy that, since philanthropy could not be counted on, "we must obtain a regular governmental subsidy." The CRB, Hoover pointed out in 1916, "is . . . almost wholly supported by Government funds. . . . I feel that if the whole engine were placed simply on a governmental basis it would be actually safer than in the hands of a volunteer body."

Nearly four out of every five dollars Hoover spent came out of government treasuries. Of the $12 million required each month to feed the Belgians, $10 million were provided by British and French officials; by the beginning of 1917 they were the source of 90 percent of the CRB's funds. In February 1917 Hoover asked Woodrow Wilson to obtain an appropriation from Congress for his organization. Two months later, the United States was at war, and, from that moment until the end of the CRB's operation, the organization's money came entirely from the U.S. government. Contrary to the impression Hoover fostered, charitable contributions from Americans constituted only 4.5 percent of the funds the CRB disbursed.

Whatever his misconceptions, Hoover had earned worldwide kudos as "the Almoner of Starving Belgium." In June 1915 the American diplomat Hugh Gibson had written his mother: "I should like to see H.C.H. run for President. He has all the qualities required—rare common sense and judgment—wonderful executive ability—and high idealism of a practical sort. The only trouble is nobody ever heard of him." No longer could that last sentence be said. Addressing his staff early in 1917, Ambassador Page remarked on the CRB: "There never was anything like it in the world before, and it is all one man and that is Hoover." Woodrow Wilson came to the same judgment. Herbert Hoover, he told his future wife, was "a great international figure." The president added, "Such men stir me deeply and make me in love with duty!"

3

Food Czar

In April 1917, shortly after the United States declared war on Germany, Hoover received the call that, over many months, he had been angling for: to return home for an important post in Washington. "The fact of the case is that . . . I have worn out my usefulness on the present job," he had confided to Ray Lyman Wilbur the previous fall. "In the upbuilding of this enterprise, . . . I have had to quarrel with a goodly number of people." Never a man of modest ambition, Hoover had sought nothing less than a position "of Cabinet rank," and he had been nagging Edward M. House and others close to Wilson to put in a good word. When the summons finally came, his assignment—"to organize . . . food activities"— was ill-defined and more constricted than what he had been seeking, but Hoover recognized that it had large possibilities, provided that he was given carte blanche.

Colonel House cautioned the president that unless Hoover was accorded "full control" he would be "unwilling to take the job, for he is the kind of man that has to have complete control in order to do the thing well." (Insistence on total dominance, House believed, was Hoover's "besetting fault.") Wilson had concluded that the democratic way to run the war mobilization was through committees, but Hoover demanded exclusive authority, "such as this democracy has never hitherto granted," over "every phase of food administration from the soil to the stomach." The president yielded and, on May 19, 1917, announced that he was asking Congress to create the position of food administrator.

Hoover had no intention of waiting until Congress got around to passing a food bill. Within days, an old Stanford chum was writing that Hoover "is booked up with interviews like a barber's chair on Saturday night." Though he directed a phantom agency with no statutory powers, Hoover acted as though he were a plenipotentiary. He immediately set up an office, recruited a staff, and issued orders. By cadging a sum from the president's discretionary fund, he put himself in the position to spend government money without congressional authority.

Aware as no administrator had been before of what a powerful force American women could be, he recruited half a million to go door-to-door enrolling housewives as "members" of a Food Administration that did not yet exist. During the first two weeks of July, nearly one hundred thousand volunteers, including Camp Fire Girls, fanned out across the country with pledge cards. In Maryland, a "Food Conservation Army," dressed, said the *Baltimore Sun*, in the "Hoover Costume"—"white shirtwaist and skirt, with the badges of their rank and the Hoover brassard on their arm band"— gave Lou Hoover a snappy military salute.

Determined to avoid the European practice of food rationing, which, in its reliance on bureaucracies and prosecution of violators, he regarded as "Prussianizing," Hoover counted on "the spirit of self-denial and self-sacrifice." A man who wore scuffed suits (always of the same dreary design) and shoes with broken laces, he could not see why anyone should covet luxuries or want to dine out. "Afternoon tea," the Kansas editor William Allen White wrote later, "was not in his social lexicon, and when he appeared at a tea he was like a Great Dane at a cat show—sniffy, but not so savage as evidently he wished to be." Hoover preached "the gospel of the clean plate": fewer meals, smaller portions. On Tuesdays, citizens were to do without meat; on Wednesdays, without bread. The Food Administration celebrated as a model of austerity a woman who had secured pledge cards from each of her ten servants: Eleanor Roosevelt, spouse of the assistant secretary of the navy.

So pervasive were the food administrator's messages that *Webster's* gained a new entry: *Hooverize*, meaning to economize in the national interest. It became a household word. A 1918 Valentine's Day card read:

> I can Hooverize on dinner,
> And on lights and fuel too,
> But I'll never learn to Hooverize,
> When it comes to loving you.

Hoover cultivated the black arts of public relations. "The world lives by phrases," he said, and "we are good advertisers." He arranged for propaganda on movie screens and persuaded clergymen to deliver sermons on the gospel of food conservation. Schoolchildren were taught to sing "The Patriotic Potato." Posters exhorted families: "Do Not Help the Hun at Meal Time" and reminded them "Wheatless days in America make sleepless nights in Germany." Women were beseeched to "cook the Kaiser's goose on their own stoves." Above all, Hoover's agency pounded home the message "Food Will Win the War."

The same principle of voluntarism infused the staffing of the Food Administration. At his own insistence, Hoover served without salary, and the only personnel receiving wages were clerks. "If it falls to my lot to control the food supply of the United States," Hoover had confided in mid-May 1917, "I shall begin at once to cut off every official and every theorist. There must be, above all, no professors on this job." The "only people in the country" whose knowledge of the field he could rely upon, he said, were the "commercial interests." Within the agency, he organized commodity divisions run by corporation minions on leave—"dollar-a-year-men" who knew who buttered their bread. More than three-quarters of a million volunteers ran the local branches. Hoover promulgated this structure as quintessentially democratic, but his reliance on unremunerated officials vested decision making in men of independent means. Devolution guaranteed control by elites. Hoover's notion of how to reach out to the countryside was to ask the biggest banker in a rural county to bring together other local power brokers to select the county food director. To farmers, that was placing foxes in chicken coops.

Hoover saw his main goal as inducing increased production, and he believed that the best way to achieve it was by offering hefty incentives. When a survey by the Federal Trade Commission found that Hoover had permitted exorbitant profits by the Big Five meatpackers, he tried to suppress the report. He also largely trusted manufacturers to discipline themselves. "The Food Administration," Hoover explained, "is called into being to stabilize and not to disturb conditions."

Yet, while singing the praises of voluntarism, he pressed for enactment of the Lever food control bill, which, one U.S. senator later protested, gave Hoover "a power such as no Caesar ever employed over a conquered province in the bloodiest days of Rome's bloody despotism." Winning a war "requires a dictatorship of some kind or another," Hoover asserted. "A democracy must submerge itself temporarily in the hands of an able man or an able group of men. No other way has ever been found." As Congress debated the measure, Hoover demanded authority to institute "forced food conservation"—including mandating meatless and wheatless days in every restaurant in America—and to penalize "the small minority of skunks" who schemed to exploit the emergency.

On August 10, 1917, Wilson, after signing the Lever Act into law, turned over the signature pen to Hoover—a welcome present on his forty-third birthday. The law, which forbade hoarding, waste, and "unjust and unreasonable" rates, authorized the president (and, by implication his surrogate, the food administrator) to require businesses to be licensed. Disobeying orders was punishable by a fine and two years in prison. With Hoover given unprecedented power to impose his will on the marketplace, his prerogatives, said the prominent rural journal *Wallace's Farmer*, were "the greatest ever held by any man in the history of the world."

No longer in limbo after three months of incertitude, Hoover still had to cope with a predicament as intractable as it had been before the Lever Act. He confronted the formidable challenge of getting farmers to grow more and grocery shoppers to buy less so that surplus food could be sent to America's overseas allies. At the same time, he dared not let this demand boost costs or create shortages in the United States. He took over at, in the phrase of the historian David M. Kennedy, "a time of giddily levitating food prices" that were riling consumers. Housewives had been looting groceries and battling police. Hoover, said one periodical, had "the biggest war job west of the trenches."

. . .

Though Hoover loathed the headline rubric "food czar," that appellation hit the mark. It was not a critic but a publicist for the Food Administration who coined the slogan "Herbert Hoover—the Autocrat of the Breakfast Table." While praising "patriotic cooperation," Hoover brandished a cudgel to hammer millers, farmers, and middlemen into submission. On October 10, 1917, he issued an edict requiring the licensing of every American who worked in any phase of the production and distribution of commodities ranging from barley to pork to fruit to fish—a decree George Nash has characterized as "perhaps the most extraordinary regulatory act ever taken by the federal government."

Hoover issued one ukase after another—to bakers on what percentage of nonwheat flour they must use, to consumers on what they had to buy if they wanted a loaf of bread—and he ordered restaurants to remove sugar bowls from their tables. "Voluntary conservation," he said, was all well and good, but the requirements of the Allies for food were "greater than can be borne upon a purely voluntary basis." In cooperation with the fuel administrator, he shut down factories for five days to reserve transportation for coal destined for Europe, and he persuaded Wilson to use his powers under the Espionage Act to embargo shipments to destinations that did not have the food czar's approval.

Routinely, Hoover circumvented the intent of Congress and exceeded his authority. The U.S. Senate had stipulated that the Food Administration could not buy or sell sugar, but that did not stop Hoover from organizing a gigantic cartel to hold prices down. Without any legal sanction, he established penalties for small retailers whose behavior he regarded as "unreasonable," and, though he had no statutory power whatsoever over farmers, he cornered the market on wheat. As head of the Food Administration's Grain Corporation with a capital of $50 million, Hoover informed millers that if they did not sell flour to the government at a price he determined, he would requisition it, and he told bakers they must make "Victory bread or close."

With each passing day, his invocations of classical economic thought became rarer. In January 1918, in response to a question from Senator Lodge, Hoover said that "the law of supply and demand" had been "suspended." Three months later, he added that "this law is not sacred. . . . Its unchecked operation might even jeopardize our success in war." It was imperative, he maintained, that "economic thinkers denude themselves of their procrustean formulas of supply and demand," for in crises "government must necessarily regulate the price, and all theories to the contrary go by the board."

To ensure adherence to his conservation directives, Hoover relied on his "one police force—the American woman." A network of 1,200 Price Interpreting Boards announced "fair prices," which were published in newspapers so that housewives might boycott any grocer or butcher who did not fall into line. "We need some phrase that puts the stamp of shame on wasteful eating, dressing and display of jewelry," Hoover said. In Indiana, regarded as the model state, self-appointed patrols invited any innkeeper or baker who did not comply with meatless and wheatless stipulations to discuss with the federal or county district attorney why he was hindering the conduct of the war.

At the same time that Hoover was imposing austerity on Americans, he was browbeating the British, French, and Italians by threatening to deny them loans from the U.S. government if they did not come to heel. America's European allies could not buy a morsel of wheat or sugar without Hoover's okay. At one point, he actually cut back food shipments to Europe in order to hold down prices at corner groceries in the United States. Hoover, who had won acclaim for feeding a neutral nation, did not hesitate a moment to clamp down on neutrals seeking to purchase food from America.

Neither abroad nor at home did Hoover endear himself to officialdom. George Creel, who headed the Committee on Public Information, recalled that Hoover spoke "only in chill monosyllables," and Colonel House became so concerned about the food administrator's attitude that he made the rounds of Washington hostesses, imploring them to "be nice to Hoover because he's not happy. He doesn't understand how to work with Congress or politicians." Hoover circulated misinformation and, when he was caught in a lie, jiggled figures to place the blame on someone else. The food administrator, concluded the British ambassador to the United States, had "no parliamentary arts" and made "very bitter enemies."

Yet well before the end of the war Hoover had emerged as an international hero. Two hundred thousand British pupils wrote him letters of thanks for food. In July 1918 King George summoned him to Buckingham Palace to express gratitude, and at a feast hosted by the lord mayor of London, the archbishop of Canterbury and other dignitaries lavished acclaim. In August Parisians cheered him as "the man who made it possible for France to eat." That summer, at the royal cottage, King Albert bestowed upon him a unique honor: "*Ami de la Nation belge*," and, as the American drove off, the monarch saluted him. In his own land, Hoover was called by Supreme Court justice Louis Brandeis "the biggest figure injected into Washington by the war."

As director of multifold operations, Hoover had been magisterial. The Allies were able to prevail in good part because they could count on food from America. Though this was his first tenure in Washington, Hoover proved remarkably adroit at bureaucratic infighting. More than once, he had gotten his way by drafting a letter augmenting his powers and handing it to the president for signature. When congressmen badgered him at hearings, Hoover, said the *New York Times*, conducted himself with "perfect sangfroid." In July 1918 a jubilant Hoover was able to report to the president that in the past year the United States had delivered over $1.4 billion worth of food to Europe. He also asserted that his policies had prevented food riots in American cities that would have resulted in "blood in our gutters."

Hoover proffered clashing explanations for his success. On one occasion, he told a congressional committee that democracy had triumphed because of "its willingness to yield to dictatorship." Customarily, however, he put forth an altogether different account, which is the one that accompanied him the rest of his days. The public-spirited American people, he claimed, had responded wholeheartedly to the request that they conserve food, demonstrating that "there was no power in autocracy equal to the voluntary effort of a free people."

This insistence on the superiority of the private realm to intervention by the state once again flew in the face of facts. Though Hoover hailed the spirit of sacrifice among consumers, improvisations like breadless days had only a marginal impact. Over many months, consumption of wheat in America actually increased, as working-class citizens largely ignored the Food Administration's propaganda. Women canvassers met more resistance than compliance. In some states, less than 10 percent of housewives signed pledge cards. Many who scribbled their names on cards did so because it was the easiest way to get rid of a caller. Moreover, Hoover, as a member of Wilson's "war cabinet," repeatedly scoffed at the notion that the free market could be counted on to allocate resources fairly. While denying that the Food Administration was "a price-fixing body," he sought "an absolutely fixed price" for essential crops, and he put the federal government in the market on such a massive scale that even he had to acknowledge it was "a sort of socialization of industry."

Though in the spring of 1917 he had told a Senate committee that the Food Administration "should die with the war," the armistice found him unwilling to surrender authority. He wanted to keep the agency alive even beyond July 1, 1919, which Congress would not permit. To feed Europe after the war, Hoover told Wilson, it was "absolutely necessary" for Congress to appropriate a sum twenty times the budget of the Food Administration. But Hoover's recurrent reliance on the state found no place in his memory bank.

. . .

In autumn 1918—at the eleventh minute of the eleventh hour of the eleventh month—the Great War ended, and five days later Hoover sailed to Europe. Earlier in November, the State Department's William Bullitt, concerned about the consequences of the disintegration of the Hapsburg empire, had urged Wilson to send the food czar to Austria because Hoover's name "carries such prestige throughout the world that the people of Austria will trust in his ability to perform the impossible, and will be inclined to await his coming before turning in despair to Bolshevism." The president had reached the same conclusion. He ordered Hoover to convert the Food Administration into an organization for relief and reconstruction on the Continent—the assignment for which Hoover had been lobbying.

In Paris, Wilson housed Hoover with members of the U.S. delegation, but instead of taking part in the wrangling at the Hall of Mirrors in Versailles, Hoover struggled, as he said, "with the gaunt realities that prowled outside." An agent of the U.S. government as head of the American Relief Administration, he served also as director-general of Relief for the Allied and Associated Powers, economic director of the Supreme Economic Council, and chair of both the Inter-Allied Food Council and the European Coal Council. He refused, though, to accept supervision from any international authority. Acting on his own, he saw to it that within days the first vessels laden with food were bound for Trieste.

Establishing missions from Helsingfors to Salonika and east to Tiflis, Hoover cut a wide swath. He controlled traffic on the Danube, Rhine, Vistula, and Elbe; coordinated railways in eighteen countries; rebuilt bridges and highways; reordered currencies; combated typhus; and reopened mines. All of these activities were in addition to his main task of finding and distributing enough food to save nearly four hundred million people from starvation. Just as ingenious as he had been earlier in Belgium, Hoover in one deal swapped two Austrian locomotives for two million Galician eggs. Before its authority expired, the American Relief Administration transported millions of tons of food, clothing, and other necessities to war victims in twenty-one nations. Earlier, even while American doughboys were dying on the western front, Hoover had announced that he was planning to feed the Germans after the war. Much to the distress of Senator Lodge, he did.

In the summer of 1919, U.S. government money for the ARA ran out, and Hoover transformed it into a private organization. The next year, he raised almost $30 million by staging "banquets" at which diners, paying $1,000 each, were served the same meager meals on the same tin dishes on which underfed waifs overseas had to make do. At the head table, a lighted candle before an empty chair represented "the invisible guest" who would be nourished by contributions from the United States. "These children," said Hoover, "are a charge on the heart of the entire world." Under the ARA, the European Children's Fund—a forerunner of CARE—fed millions in an arc from Armenia to Finland. The Finns added a new word to their lexicon: to *hoover* means to help.

The ARA did not act wholly from humanitarian motives. With the armistice, Hoover, who had been laboring mightily to expand production of food during the war, abruptly found himself confronting the reverse problem: mountainous surpluses, which, he told Colonel House, constituted "a situation of utmost danger." The relief program permitted him to dump overseas these huge stock-piles valued at as much as $3 billion. Historians dispute the extent to which Hoover used providing or withholding food as a weapon to suppress Bolshevism, but there is no doubt that he did so against an attempted monarchist coup in Hungary, where he demanded the removal of Archduke Joseph and "the formation of a ministry representing labor and socialist middle classes and peasants." In Poland he moderated the military dictatorship of Józef Pilsudski by threatening to deny food unless the marshal appointed the pi-anist Ignacy Paderewski premier.

Hoover refused to be swept up in right-wing zealotry. Though he denounced Bolshevik "jackals" and thought Russia to be a "cesspool," he warned Wilson that military intervention would cre-ate "infinite harm" because it would "make us a party to establish-ing the reactionary classes in their economic domination over the lower classes," which "is against our fundamental national spirit." Moreover, if U.S. forces interceded, they would, he foresaw, be bogged down in Russia for years, and American soldiers might be-come infected with the Bolshevik virus.

Hoover also viewed warily the transactions at Versailles. In Feb-ruary 1917, a day after Germany began unrestricted submarine warfare, he had confided: "If we have got to go into this war, I am extremely anxious that we should not go into it in alliance with anybody. . . . I dread the horrible entanglement of this country with all of the objectives of certain of the allies." He opposed any postwar collaboration that failed to concede America's economic preeminence, and he was dismayed by many of the treaty provi-sions. After Wilson returned to the United States, Colonel House wrote him that Hoover "is simply reveling in gloom. He gives Eu-rope but thirty days longer of orderly life—after that, it is to be revolution, starvation and chaos."

The differences between the Old World and the New, Hoover ultimately concluded, represented "the collision of civilizations that had grown three hundred years apart." The United States, he believed, "was the only nation since the time of the Crusades that had fought other peoples' wars for ideals." In contrast, Europe, "a furnace of hate" and "a boiling social and economic caldron," spread "miasmic infections." In April 1919 he wrote Wilson: "If the Allies cannot be brought to adopt peace on the basis of the 14 points, we should retire from Europe lock, stock, and barrel, and we should lend to the whole world our economic and moral strength, or the world will swim in a sea of misery and disaster worse than the dark ages." When Hoover's ship docked in New York five months later, he told the press that he was turning his back on Europe and hoped never to see it again.

Congenitally lugubrious though he was, Hoover gained the admiration of a perceptive British commentator for his insights. Herbert Hoover, wrote John Maynard Keynes, was "the only man who emerged from the ordeal of Paris with an enhanced reputation." Keynes added:

> This complex personality, with his habitual air of weary Titan (or as others might put it, of exhausted prize fighter), his eyes steadily fixed on the true and essential facts of the European situation, imported into the Councils of Paris . . . precisely that atmosphere of reality, knowledge, magnanimity and disinterestedness which, if they had been found in other quarters also, would have given us the Good Peace.

Despite his misgivings, Hoover quite unexpectedly announced that he strongly favored speedy ratification of the Versailles treaty—including the creation of the League of Nations, which, "for good or ill," was embedded in the document. He did so not out of any utopian expectation that Tennyson's vision in "Locksley Hall" of a "Parliament of Man" would be realized in Geneva, but because "until peace is made, Europe cannot get back to work." In October 1919 he delivered speeches warning that delay would foster unrest and would deprive the United States of overseas markets. Dead set against engaging in any "mission of international justice," he nonetheless maintained that Americans could "no longer" keep up "the pretense of an insularity that we do not possess."

. . .

The aftermath of war found Hoover at sixes and sevens. "I don't want to be just a rich man," he confided to the novelist Mary Austin. Maybe he could publish a newspaper, or perhaps promote a mining school. "Things came up in his mind," she wrote, "and turned over, showing white bellies like fish in a net." One thing was certain: whatever he did would be in the private sector. He had "drunk of the bitterness of public life to such a depth," he said, "that no inducement short of national danger" could entice him again into government.

Yet when Hoover was mentioned as a prospect for the presidency in 1920, he sent conflicting signals. In 1919 he told a former colleague who wanted him to run that "the whole idea fills my soul with complete revulsion." He did not think he could be nominated; he did not have "the mental attitude or the politician's manner"; and he was "too sensitive to political mud." In his diary, though, Colonel House recorded his pleasure that Hoover "did not pretend to me that he was not interested in the country-wide movement to make him President. It is patent that he has been working overtime in that direction."

Hoover's actions and statements made him especially appealing to progressives. During the war, he had urged Wilson to push for a tax on excess profits, and he had rebuked Social Darwinists by saying that "civilization spells the protection of the helpless. . . . The survival of the strong, the development of the individual, must be tempered, or else we return two thousand years in our civilization." While carrying on a cordial dialogue with the head of the American Federation of Labor, Samuel Gompers, he told the Boston Chamber of Commerce that "industry must be humanized" and the workforce "regarded not merely as a cost of production, but as a living agent, with human instincts and social wants." As vice chairman of the Second Industrial Conference that convened in

December 1919, Hoover advocated a department of public works, a federal employment service, and home-loan banks; after the meetings ended in March 1920, he was chief author of a report to the president recommending a minimum wage, a forty-eight-hour workweek, the eradication of child labor, improved housing, and equal pay for men and women.

Though the possibility of the infiltration of America by Bolshevik agents alarmed him, Hoover expressed dismay at "transgressions against real civil liberty by the use of war powers in peace." He deplored injunctions against strikes, "non-trial by jury of reds," and the expulsion of legally elected Socialist legislators in New York State. He admonished Attorney General A. Mitchell Palmer and other patrioteers that communism fed on exploitation. "We shall never remedy justifiable discontent until we eradicate the misery which ruthless individualism has imposed upon a minority," he said. More troubled by the right than by the left, he observed that "radicalism is blatant and displays itself in the open," while "reaction too often fools the people through subtle channels of obstruction."

Not surprisingly, given these views, a host of progressives promoted Hoover for the presidency. "I think he is precisely the man that the liberal movement in America, as you and I understand it, needs," one progressive former mayor of an Ohio city wrote another Buckeye mayor. "His hardness is all on the surface." To Hoover's standard rallied the muckrakers Ida Tarbell and Ray Stannard Baker and both of the country's leading liberal journals. "Many a great reputation that was won in the war is crumbling, or has already crumbled," wrote Oswald Garrison Villard. "We believe Mr. Hoover's will grow as time passes. The *Nation* is proud, indeed, that so true an American has served humanity so conspicuously and beyond all gratitude well." In like vein, the *New Republic* editors Herbert Croly and Walter Lippmann called Hoover "a Providential gift to the American people for the office of pilot during the treacherous navigation of the next few years."

Progressives, though, did not hold a monopoly on ardor for

Hoover. So inundated was the conservative *Boston Herald* with letters that in January 1920 it announced, "For the present, at least, we propose to print in the Mail Bag no more individual opinions favorable to the presidential nomination of Herbert Hoover." Devotion to Hoover united the publishers of the Main Street magazines *Saturday Evening Post* and *Ladies' Home Journal* with the laborite Heywood Broun and the Manhattan sophisticates Dorothy Parker and Robert Benchley. A poll of the Harvard faculty favored him two to one. Unrecognized save in mining circles in 1914, his name—which appeared on every restaurant menu during the war—was more familiar to newspaper readers by 1920 than that of any American save Wilson. Especially beguiling was the legend of his rise from rags to riches. "Hoover," the historian Paul Glad has written, "seemed to have come striding into public consciousness directly from the pages of a Horatio Alger novel."

One enthusiastic letter to Hoover—from a well-known Harvard economist—unwittingly raised a bothersome issue, however. He would cast his ballot for the former food czar, Frank Taussig said, "on any ticket whatever, republican, democratic, new faith, socialistic, or Bolshevik." That jocular promise pointed up an intriguing question: if Hoover did run for president in 1920, which party's banner would he carry?

Colonel House was not the only Wilsonian to claim him for the Democrats. "He is certainly a wonder, and I wish we could make him President of the United States," said the assistant secretary of the navy, Franklin Delano Roosevelt. "There would not be a better one." His wife agreed. Eleanor Roosevelt thought Hoover "the only man I know who . . . [has] first hand knowledge of European questions and great organizing ability and understands business . . . not only from the capitalistic point of view but also from the workers' standpoint."

Hoover, though, trod water. Raised in a Republican milieu, he had joined the Republican Club of New York City in 1909. Furthermore, not all Democrats thought he was a good fit. Since, after some qualms, he had concluded that the president had to accept reservations in order to get the Versailles treaty approved, he could no longer be regarded as a true Wilsonian. The president himself had come to distrust him. "I have the feeling that he would rather see a good cause fail than succeed if he were not the head of it," Wilson said. Most important, Hoover recognized that the Democrats were expected to lose badly in 1920, and he did not want to be their sacrificial lamb.

For a long while, Hoover maintained that he had no partisan affiliation. When a prominent Democrat wooed him, he responded by denouncing both parties, revealing "a disdain for political organizations," the Democrat noted in his diary, "which is likely to lead him to trouble." Hoover informed Colonel House that he could not take up with the Democrats because of the party's southern reactionary element, and he could not tag himself a Republican because of the mossbacks in the East. (In 1917 he had resigned from Manhattan's Republican Club.) In February 1920, he stated, "There are about forty live issues in this country in which I am interested, and before I can answer whether I am a Democrat or Republican, I shall have to know how each party stands on these issues."

Not until March 30, 1920, did he announce that he was a Republican—in a snotty statement guaranteed to antagonize GOP stalwarts:

> If the Republican party with the independent element of which I am naturally affiliated, adopts a forward-looking, liberal, constructive platform on the Treaty and on our economic issues, and if the party proposes measures for sound business administration of the country, and is neither reactionary nor radical in its approach to our great domestic questions, and is backed by men who undoubtedly assure the consummation of these policies and measures, I will give it my entire support. While I do not, and will not myself, seek the nomination, if it is felt that the issues necessitate it and it is demanded of me, I can not refuse service.

That declaration did not serve him well. After taking the high ground that he could not identify with a party until he knew its candidate and its platform, he had, in an irritatingly self-serving manner, abruptly committed himself without knowing either. "In effect," commented the *New York Times*, "Mr. Hoover tells the Republican party he would like to belong to [it] if [it] will be the kind of party to which he would like to belong. And that, if he belongs to it, he would have no objection to leading it."

The GOP extended a less than hearty welcome. Little more than a year before, he had been denounced by the Republican National Committee for asserting, "We must have united support for the President," a statement regarded as a plea to voters to choose Democrats in the 1918 midterm elections. Hoover, announced the head of the Republican Congressional Committee, was guilty of "prostitution of official station." Nor was hostility confined to the Old Guard. Hoover's performance when food czar, the influential farm editor Henry C. Wallace said, "gave evidence of a mental bias which causes farmers to thoroughly distrust him. They look upon him as a typical autocrat of big business." Of the many presidential aspirants in 1920, the Grange announced, Hoover was "the most objectionable to the farmers of this country."

In these unpropitious circumstances, Hoover still found it hard to let go of the phantasm that he might be the Republican choice. A Stanford friend noted that Hoover had written Herbert Jr., "[My] nomination for the Presidency would be a great deal like [your] flivver. It would take a lot of people to start it, would make a lot of noise, and they would all have to walk back home in the end." Rashly, though, he permitted his name to be entered in the California Republican primary against the favorite son, Senator Hiram Johnson.

Hoover never had a chance. Right-wing Republicans disowned him, and liberals remembered that Johnson had been Teddy Roosevelt's running mate on the Progressive ticket in 1912. A longtime foe of the trusts, Johnson charged that Hoover was "backed by the great powerful business interests to which he pandered while he was Food Administrator." In addition, Hoover's opponents capitalized on uneasiness about his many years in London. Mock posters read "Vote for 'Erbert 'Oover," in tune with a Missouri senator's reference to Hoover as a "recent acquisition to our population." Without campaigning, Hoover polled 200,000 votes, but he fell far short of Johnson's 370,000 in the May primary. All hopes that he might be a presidential contender that year were at an end. From his position at the command post in the Savoy ballroom in 1914, he had moved—despite an extraordinary record of achievement—to the role of bystander in 1920.

When Republicans that summer settled on an egregiously lackluster presidential nominee, they confronted Hoover with a difficult question—whether a pro-League progressive could support the nationalist conservative Warren Harding. Hoover might have fallen into line quietly by reasoning that the Democratic ticket of James M. Cox and Franklin D. Roosevelt did not offer a spectacularly better option and that no one could expect him to bolt so soon from a party in which he had just reenlisted. But Hoover would never permit himself to appear as anything but righteous. He insisted, against all evidence, that a vote for Harding was an endorsement of the League and that the Wilson administration in which he had been a prominent figure was "in the main reactionary" and "since the armistice . . . a failure by all the tests that we can apply." (Hoover, Wilson retorted, was "no friend" of his, "and I do not care to do anything to assist him in any way in any undertaking whatever.") His rationale could not have been lamer and in some quarters earned him contempt. Yet in one important respect Hoover had come off well. He had positioned himself to be a deserving recipient of Harding's largesse, should he be disposed to reenter the public realm.

4

Commerce

After his landslide victory, President-elect Harding announced that he was going to consult the "best minds" in the nation on how to compose his cabinet, but he needed no prompting about one obvious selection. He told a friend, "Reily, do you know, taking Herbert Hoover up one side and down the other, and taking into consideration the knowledge he has of things generally, I believe he's the smartest gink I know." Harding determined that Hoover could have his choice: either the Interior or the Commerce portfolio. Weeks before election day, William Allen White had anticipated the invitation. "If I were Hoover, I would do it," he said, for Harding "is a man who is going to take the color of his environment and Hoover could help make an environment."

Harding, though, found Hoover a hard sell. Republican Anglophobes and isolationists—some of them progressives—regarded Hoover as a Wilsonian infidel on foreign policy. Right-wingers thought him unsound on domestic issues. "Hoover," confided a powerful GOP senator, "gives most of us gooseflesh." Hoover was painfully conscious of this disapproval. He saw no point in getting embroiled in a donnybrook over as backwater a department as Commerce, and the Interior post did not appeal to him. Furthermore, he had lucrative prospects in the private sector, including an approach from the international financier Paul Warburg. Accordingly, he drafted a letter to Harding on December 22, 1920, that began with the comment, "I cannot but be aware that there is opposition in certain politically-minded quarters," and ended with a request "that you will dismiss from your mind all thought of my appointment."

The president-elect, however, would not be denied. He informed two Pennsylvania senators who were pushing Andrew Mellon to be secretary of the Treasury that he would agree to name the Pittsburgh multimillionaire only if they abandoned their objections to Hoover. Grudgingly, they knuckled under. On February 12, 1921, Harding made a formal offer. Hoover hesitated, not least because the industrialist Daniel Guggenheim had asked him to take part in mining ventures at a guaranteed annual income of half a million dollars. When Hoover finally accepted the cabinet position, less than two weeks before Harding's inauguration, he did so on his own terms, saying haughtily that the Department of Commerce "as it stands today . . . offers no field for constructive national service equal to that I already occupy in private life." He wanted it strictly understood that bureaus would be taken away from other departments and given to him and, as he wrote later in his *Memoirs*, that his warrant would cover nothing less than "business, agriculture, labor, finance, and foreign affairs."

Though the elevation of Hoover to the cabinet pleased progressives, some commentators wondered whether, as secretary of commerce, he would not quickly fade from view. Hoover, stated the *New Republic*, was "easily the most constructive man in public life." But another journalist believed that he was "eclipsed by a preceding fame. . . . The War spoiled life . . . for Hoover. After its magnificent amplifications of personality, it is hard to descend to every day, and be not a tremendous figure, but a successful secretary of an unromantic department." Hoover's only duties as secretary of commerce, a predecessor told him, would be "putting the fish to bed at night and turning on the lights around the coast."

. . .

Hoover had much grander notions. Unlike conservatives, who wanted to shrink the federal government, he was an empire builder. He greatly increased appropriations for his department; set up three new bureaus (aeronautics, radio, and housing); and extended his activities into realms that bore only the most tangential relationship to "commerce," such as recreation. So expansively did he interpret his mandate that he has been titled "the grand marshal of economic policy at home as abroad."

He made the Bureau of Foreign and Domestic Commerce under Julius Klein, a Harvard professor of Latin American history and economics, the linchpin of the department—sextupling its appropriations. The bureau conducted censuses of market behavior in American cities that no European country would institute for another thirty years and posted commercial representatives in cities from Riga, Latvia, to Soerabaja, East Java. In *Caravans of Commerce* (1926), a book dedicated to Hoover, the freelance journalist Isaac Marcosson painted a glamorous portrait of the bureau: "Its attachés have risked the glaciers of the Andes, and braved the fevers of Ecuador; they have been wrecked on the headwaters of the Amazon; they have encountered bandits beyond the Great Wall of China, all to the end that fresh fields be opened up for the products of American farm and factory."

In aggrandizing his empire, the sky was not the limit. Hoover approved a large role for the U.S. government in aviation, not because he favored a nanny state but because federal inspection of planes and licensing of pilots would lower insurance rates and encourage travelers to risk boarding aircraft. Opposed to the European pattern of government-funded airlines, he wanted Washington to limit itself to an indirect subsidy by turning delivery of airmail over to private firms—especially after thirty-one of the first forty pilots employed by the government to ferry mail died in crashes. For the industry to flourish, Orville Wright testified, the government had to provide facilities such as emergency landing fields. Hoover went beyond that advice by requiring all runways to be equipped with lights and radio beams. To expand the market for planes, the newly created aeronautics branch advertised their value to farmers for crop dusting. When the nation's capital had to come up with an appropriate name for its first airport, it chose "Hoover Field."

Hoover seized control of the air in a different sense by moving in on another infant industry: radio. When his tenure began, there were only two stations, both dabblers; a year later, there were 320, emitting a cacophony of sounds. Through edicts that he had no authority to issue or that were forbidden by an act of Congress, he imposed regularity. To lessen congestion, he ordered all amateurs off the airwaves; he empowered himself to issue licenses; and, in contravention of both domestic and international law, he assigned frequencies. In 1925 the department suspended the license of Aimee Semple McPherson's radio outlet in California for straying from its assignment. The popular evangelist wired Hoover: "Please order your minions of Satan to leave my station alone. You cannot expect the Almighty to abide by your wavelength nonsense. When I offer my prayers to Him, I must fit in with His wave reception." But Hoover prevailed, even though Congress denied him "the Napoleonic powers," in the phrase of one critic, that he sought. Hoover left posterity two legacies: Marconi's marvelous invention would not be operated by public institutions but by privately owned (and lightly regulated) networks—the bigger the better— and these corporations would profit by inflicting commercials on listeners. In the Hoover years, as the president of RCA said, the "heresy of government ownership, especially in radio matters," was exorcised.

Disturbed by reports that as much as one-third of the American people lived in inferior homes, Hoover established a housing division that drafted model zoning statutes and a model housing code, and he exhorted builders to lower costs. Inadequate shelter, he maintained, was "thriving food for Bolshevism." A conference he called led to the creation of an American Construction Council, which sought to develop industry standards—but also to combat government regulation. Convinced that he needed someone of esteem to head the council, Hoover asked Franklin D. Roosevelt, who readily agreed. But when FDR pressed him to herd recalcitrant firms into line, Hoover flatly refused. As a result, the council foundered.

While burrowing into new fields, Hoover never forgot that his main responsibility as commerce secretary was to serve American business, though always with an eye on how to improve it. With his encouragement, the Bureau of the Census in July 1921 launched *Survey of Current Business*, an invaluable monthly periodical. Hoover believed, at a time when economic intelligence was primitive, that publishing statistics would stabilize the market by diminishing overstocking and allaying unreasonable anxiety about economic conditions. In addition, it would benefit small businesses, which could not afford to search out the information that their bigger rivals could pay to get. Data were not gathered by the government but provided by trade associations, which were self-interested. Nonetheless, the *Survey* was an important innovation.

The Bureau of Standards, which under Hoover earned a reputation as "the largest research laboratory in the world," housed a division of simplified commercial practice to pursue his preoccupation with efficiency. He knew that to the apparently easy question, "What are the dimensions of a one-inch board?" a government committee found no fewer than thirty-two answers. To simplify, the division—which arranged more than 1,200 conferences—slashed varieties of everything from bedsprings to milk bottles. (Ironically, in his war against duplication, Hoover created so many committees that they duplicated one another's work.) The government never decreed the elimination of superfluous models; it only recommended. Still, Hoover let businessmen know that if they were going to bid on government contracts they had better meet federal specifications. He also convened a National Conference on Street and Highway Safety, which favored imposing order on automobile traffic by requiring uniform signs: red for stop, green for go.

To critics who accused Hoover of homogenization, he retorted

that the "man who has a standard automobile, a standard telephone, a standard bathtub, a standard electric light, a standard radio, and one and one-half hours less average daily labor is more of
a man and has a fuller life and more individuality than he has without them." In the spirit of Henry Ford, who said that a customer
could buy a flivver in any color so long as it was black, Hoover told
the novelist Sherwood Anderson, a critic of Babbittry, "When I go
to ride in an automobile, it does not matter to me that there are a
million other automobiles on the road just like mine. I am going
somewhere and I want to get there in what comfort I can and at
the lowest cost."

• • •

Not content with his spacious realm in Commerce, Hoover set his
eyes on the domains of his cabinet colleagues. He gave Harding a
reorganization syllabus transferring to Commerce segments of two
independent regulatory commissions and all or part of seventeen
agencies currently lodged in other departments. Information collection, he insisted, was solely his prerogative. Hence, the Department of Agriculture's Bureau of Markets should yield to his
Bureau of the Census, and Commerce should take over the Labor
Department's Bureau of Labor Statistics. When he did not get his
way in either instance, he acted as though he had. Stiff resistance
prevented him from absorbing Agriculture's Bureau of Public
Roads and Interior's Geological Survey and U.S. Land Office, but
he did grab the Bureau of Mines and the Patent Office from Interior and snatched the Bureau of Customs Statistics from Mellon's
Treasury.

Hoover did not even hesitate to challenge Secretary of State
Charles Evans Hughes, who had come within a few votes of being
elected president in 1916 and whose appearance was likened to
that of Jove. Hughes regarded overseas affairs as wholly in his do-
minion, whereas Hoover insisted that anything economic in nature
belonged to him. To a remarkable extent, Hoover made his presence felt in the conduct of foreign affairs. At the Washington naval

arms conference in 1921, he counseled Hughes on Asian policy, and as chair of the Inter-American High Commission—a post traditionally belonging to the secretary of the Treasury—he delved into financial relations in the Western Hemisphere. Hoover, who held on to his Commerce post when Calvin Coolidge rose to the presidency after Harding's death in 1923, did not hesitate to denounce Coolidge's intervention in Nicaragua with marines or to criticize U.S. dollar diplomacy in Mexico. He also spoke out on immigration: he advocated exclusion of Japanese, since there were "biological and cultural grounds why there should be no mixture of Oriental and Caucasian blood," and he deplored admitting Puerto Ricans ("undersized Latins") at a time when quotas restricted the entry of "Nordics."

With the world as his arena, the secretary of commerce took it upon himself to wage war on foreign cartels. Although he had no qualms about the very high Fordney-McCumber tariff, which created a formidable barrier for European businesses seeking to sell their goods in America, he viewed manipulation of markets by other governments as unconscionable. He attacked a Franco-German potash syndicate, whose menace he exaggerated, and, to foil Brazil's scheme to jack up the cost of coffee, he cut off loans to São Paulo and prompted the creation of a national coffee association in the United States. His biggest battle was with John Bull. When the British colonial secretary Winston Churchill fathered a scheme to boost the world price of rubber, Hoover, concerned about the impact on the vital U.S. automobile industry, struck back. By prodding Firestone and other tire makers to expand rubber plantations in Africa and Asia and by encouraging conservation measures, he drove down the price of rubber from $1.21 to 40¢ a pound. His actions took a bit of the edge off the long-standing charge that he was a craven Anglophile.

While attending to his manifold duties at Commerce, Hoover continued to head the American Relief Administration, which sped food to famine-sufferers in Soviet Russia. Throughout his life, he fiercely opposed recognition of the USSR, but when, at a public

gathering, a woman charged that American aid buttressed Bolshevism, he got up and, pounding his fist on a table, shouted, "Twenty
million people are starving. Whatever their politics, they shall be
fed!" From the September day in 1921 when the SS *Phoenix*, carrying seven hundred tons of food, sailed into Petrograd through all of
1922 and into 1923, Hoover's ARA sustained fifteen million people daily. He carried out this vast enterprise with a small cadre of
Americans, most of them unpaid—again assuring him that, in crisis, the country could rely on dedicated volunteers.

The consequences of this endeavor were double-edged. Maxim
Gorky wrote Hoover: "In the past year you have saved from death
three and one-half million children, five and one-half million
adults. . . . In the history of practical humanitarianism I know of
no accomplishment which in . . . magnitude and generosity can be
compared to the relief that you have actually accomplished." Decades later, Aleksandr Solzhenitsyn lauded the American effort in
the Volga region in almost the same words. But the operation also
had an outcome that Hoover neither intended nor welcomed.
George Kennan concluded that Hoover's benefaction had "impor-
tantly aided" the Kremlin, "not just in its economic undertakings,
but in its political prestige and capacity for survival."

These forays into international affairs led Hoover to clash with
Hughes, Mellon, and even the president. They all believed that the
government was duty-bound to safeguard overseas investments,
while Hoover wanted to ensure that businessmen did not take risks
that might require armed intervention by U.S. forces. He maintained that bankers, instead of being at liberty to invest abroad
however they pleased, required government guidance. Loans, he argued, should go only for "reproductive" activities, never for arma-
ments, but he could not get Coolidge or Mellon to agree to
regulate lending.

Mellon, who thought Hoover "too officious" and "too much an
engineer," also resented his meddling in other affairs in the purview
of the Treasury. Hoover favored taxing the securities holdings of

the "well-to-do" at a higher rate than what he deemed "earned" income. The less well-off, he believed, should pay no taxes at all, and he opposed excises on necessities. "I would like to see," he declared, "a steeply graduated tax on legacies and gifts . . . for the deliberate purpose of disintegrating large fortunes." Mellon decried these heretical views.

As secretary of commerce, Hoover also advanced the cause of conservation—traditionally the bailiwick of the secretary of the interior. He intervened to preserve the natural assets of Niagara Falls; organized a conference to save Chesapeake Bay; attempted to halt the diminution of Alaska's salmon fisheries; and prided himself on being "the arch anti-pollutionist in the country." Concerned about oil slicks fouling oceans, bays, and estuaries, he demanded "very drastic regulation" and expressed disappointment when Congress yielded to oil tycoons in eviscerating "my pollution bill." But because federal regulation was much too light-handed, Hoover failed to curb contamination of rivers and lakes, and, in Alaska, salmon runs faltered. He did better as chair of a Colorado River Commission. Under his leadership, the agency worked out water sharing among seven quarrelsome states that made possible an ambitious project in Boulder Canyon that later bore the name Hoover Dam.

No controversy over Hoover's attempts to set policy in other fields aroused nearly so much animosity as his bitter feud with the secretary of agriculture, Henry C. Wallace, who despised him. Wallace thought Hoover "bloodless," "stuffy," and "opinionated." He also believed—with good reason—that Hoover had nothing worthwhile to say to the beleaguered farmer. Hoover was willing to support measures such as the Agricultural Credits Act, which he had a hand in drafting, but he held so romanticized a view of commercial agriculture that he feared for the souls of farmers if the government intervened further. Hoover made such a mark on farm issues, however, that when Wallace died in 1924, Coolidge offered him the post of secretary of agriculture. Hoover turned the president down, but he continued, as secretary of commerce, to exert

greater influence than anyone else on Coolidge's vetoes of farm
subsidy legislation.

. . .

For a secretary of commerce, Hoover exercised extraordinary authority over the country's working conditions. When coal miners
went out on strike in 1922, Harding designated him—not the secretary of labor—as chief negotiator with the operators. The president did so because Hoover, who could speak with the prestige of
a man with a generation of experience in finance, also had won the
confidence of union leaders. Hoover commonly concluded that labor was more reasonable than management. He favored agreements
stipulating that the fruits of greater efficiency go to "the provision
of unemployment and sickness insurance . . . on an adequate scale,"
with the residue "administered through the major voice of organized
labor," and, at a time when many industrialists were promoting the
open shop, he expressed contempt for union busters.

It took a while for workers to realize that Hoover was a less than
dependable ally. Although he endorsed the right to "employee
representation," he did not distinguish between independent labor
organizations and shop councils. When employers converted these
councils into subservient company unions, Hoover raised no objection. At one point he even advocated using scabs to mine coal. He
believed that employers should pay high wages, less because he em-
pathized with workers than because he understood that there was
no point in producing goods unless there were consumers who
could afford to buy them. Furthermore, if employees were under-
paid, they might walk off their jobs, and strikes were messy. Every
major industry ought to be unionized, he told Gompers, but he had
in mind the housebroken AFL craft unions that kept their members
corralled, and he frowned on militant tactics to organize workers in
factories. "Our nation is very fortunate in having the American Federation of Labor," he declared, because radical elements "have been
met in the front line trenches by the Federation . . . and routed at
every turn." Still, he believed that there was "no economic failure so

terrible in its import as that of a country possessing a surplus of every necessity of life in which numbers willing and anxious to work are deprived of dire necessities. It simply cannot be if our moral and economic system is to survive."

When unemployment passed four million in August 1921 during a postwar recession, it was not the secretary of labor but Hoover who pushed Harding to convene a national forum to enlist support for maintaining wage levels and speeding construction. Throughout his public career, Hoover touted conferences as the democratic way—to avoid top-down decision making and to allow all voices to be heard. In truth, more often, conferences were vehicles for Hoover to impose his will. In 1921 he picked out the participants, set the agenda, chaired sessions, and wrote the findings—before the delegates had even met one another. "At the conference on unemployment, which was Mr. Hoover's," said one commentator, "the best and only example of the unemployed present was the Secretary of Labor."

A number of historians have seen Hoover's performance at these meetings as the origin of federal assumption of responsibility for countercyclical planning, but it was considerably less than that. Warning against "governmental doles and other fallacious remedies based upon the practices of European governments," Hoover told the delegates it was "not consonant with the spirit of institutions of the American people that a demand should be made upon the public treasury for the solution of every difficulty." The conferees did favor accelerating public works, but only if they were "on a 'commercial' basis, not a 'relief' basis," and they dumped the burden for getting them under way on mayors and communities. In the months after the gathering broke up, the Commerce Department served as little more than a cheerleader to local officials.

Hoover, who ended the conference by telling the delegates that their actions marked a "milestone in the progress of social thought," boasted ever after that his agitation had brought the country out of the 1921–23 recession, inaugurating an era of vibrant prosperity. The post-parley committee under the former New

York police commissioner Colonel Arthur Woods, Hoover initially claimed, had put 1 to 1.5 million to work. "Distress prevailed in every city, soup lines had been formed," he reported in 1924. Then, following the conference, "Credit and Confidence were restored in the business world. . . . And the whole country mobilized to provide emergency employment."

In fact, there is no evidence that Hoover's venture had any impact. New York City behaved as though it had never heard of his organization, and, as the historian Irving Bernstein pointed out, in one-industry towns such as Gary, Indiana, "no committee could find jobs that did not exist." Yet by 1928 Hoover had carried his self-delusion and self-promotion to the point of declaring that "within a year we restored . . . five million workers to employment." Unhappily, the lesson he again drew was that in the event of a future depression one could confidently count upon community effort for salvation.

Throughout his tenure in the Commerce Department, Hoover made labor issues part of his mandate. In 1922 he angered railway executives by asking them for a minor concession to salvage something for a shopmen's union that had called an ill-fated strike. When the owners made clear that they intended to smash the union, he said that "their social instinct belonged to an early Egyptian period." After Harry Daugherty obtained a flagrantly overreaching injunction against the union—a decree, Hoover said, that "outraged" him "by its obvious transgression of the most rudimentary rights of man"—he tongue-lashed the attorney general at a cabinet meeting.

For more than two years, Hoover brought relentless pressure on steel magnates to end barbaric twelve-hour shifts, seven days a week, in the mills. He massed figures to show that a change could be made without economic loss, but the steel barons dismissed his views as purblind and "unsocial." The twelve-hour day, they insisted, "was not of itself an injury to the employees, physically, mentally, or morally." At one point, Hoover composed a letter for Harding to send, which the president thought much too truculent.

Hoover then persuaded Harding to summon the manufacturers to the White House, and, when they proved recalcitrant, he inflamed public opinion by leaking an account of their attitude to the press. When their leader, Elbert "Judge" Gary, still balked, Harding sent him a letter, drafted by Hoover, which compelled him to capitulate.

Hoover's most conspicuous intervention in labor policy came in 1924 when, in collaboration with the United Mine Workers' chief John L. Lewis, he forged an agreement in the coal industry. After this compact was negotiated, an exultant Hoover claimed credit, but when operators repeatedly violated it, he would do nothing to see that it was carried out and, instead, began to attack the union. The rift revealed a fundamental difference of purpose. For Lewis, the key consideration was wage level; for Hoover, labor peace—so that output, which is what he cared most about, would be maintained. Nonetheless, Hoover continued to have Lewis's approbation.

. . .

His singular incursions into other jurisdictions—State, Interior, Treasury, Agriculture, Justice, Labor—elicited the well-circulated quip that Hoover was "Secretary of Commerce and Under-Secretary of all other departments." In 1925 a *New Republic* columnist expressed a similar view:

It is certainly not generally recognized . . . how extraordinarily extensive is his impress upon the government outside of his own Department. There is reason to doubt whether in the whole history of the American government a Cabinet officer has engaged in such wide diversity of activities or covered quite so much ground.

The plain fact is that no vital problem, whether in the foreign or the domestic field, arises in this administration in the handling of which Mr. Hoover does not have a real—and very often a leading—part. There is more Hoover in the administration than anyone else . . . more Hoover . . . than there is Coolidge.

Hoover's feisty behavior also helps account for why he had not a friend in the cabinet. Unable to understand how anyone could disagree with him, he flew into tantrums when men he did not think were his equals raised objections. He had a high regard for the secretary of state, whom he thought the ablest man in the cabinet—always excepting, of course, himself—but their relationship was "Mister Hughes" and "Mister Hoover." Coolidge could not stand Hoover's meddling or his presumptuousness. "What's our wonder boy done now?" the president inquired. As his time in the White House was running out, Coolidge said of Hoover, "That man has offered me unsolicited advice for six years, all of it bad!"

Despite his hyperactivity in Washington, Hoover strongly disapproved of the leviathan state. In 1921 he asked whether European currency difficulties might not be resolved by a consortium of bankers, thereby eliminating any occasion for a political response. In 1925 he told Iowa farmers that experience had taught him that "every time we find solution outside of government we have not only strengthened character but we have preserved our sense of real self government." In his hostility to bureaucracy, Hoover showed no awareness that he was not only the premier bureaucrat of the decade but the man most responsible for swollen government agencies. What began as a strong predilection ended as catechism. By 1928 he was saying, "Even if governmental conduct of business could give us more efficiency instead of less efficiency, the fundamental objection to it would remain unaltered and unabated."

Hoover, though, placed his faith not in the freewheeling entrepreneur, but in federal encouragement of trade associations, which he thought of as self-regulating entities like medieval guilds. "While I am not a believer in extending the bureaucratic functions of the Government," he explained, "I am a strong believer in the Government intervening to induce active co-operation in the community itself." He put Commerce at the disposal of existing trade associations and nudged unorganized industries to coalesce. "We are passing from a period of extreme individualistic action into a period of associational activities," he announced in 1924.

For a time, his promotion of trade associations embroiled him in a squabble with Attorney General Daugherty. Stringent enforcement of antitrust laws against trade associations was a "perversion of justice," Hoover contended. "Men have murdered with brickbats," he remarked, "but that is no reason for prohibiting brick houses." He stopped short of advocating cartels, however, stating, "I would not propose price-fixing in any form short of again reentering the trenches in another World War."

Hoover diverged from free marketers, too, in challenging classical economic theory. In 1923 he wrote: "We are constantly reminded by some . . . economists and businessmen that the fluctuation of the business cycle is inevitable; that there is an ebb and flow in the demand for commodities and services that cannot from the nature of things be regulated. I have great doubts whether there is a real foundation for this view." He denied that periodic mass unemployment was tolerable, and he believed that government had an important assignment in preventing downturns, since the market was untrustworthy. In 1928 he urged a gathering of governors to create a $3 billion reserve fund for public works "to ward off unemployment in lean years." In this instance, his conception of the need for long-range planning exceeded that of some progressives. "We had better let God run it as in the past," said Senator George Norris of Nebraska, "and not take power away from him and give it to Hoover."

Commentators found Hoover's mild iconoclasm much less germane than his rationalizations of the status quo. In an address to the U.S. Chamber of Commerce in 1924, Hoover declared: "Our homemade Bolshevist-minded critics to the contrary, the whole economic structure of our nation and the survival of our . . . levels of comfort are dependent upon the maintenance and development of leadership in the world of industry and commerce." Businessmen, he added, "deserve high public esteem." Two years earlier, he had told the National Association of Manufacturers: "There is no regulatory function in the Department of Commerce, . . . and it is my feeling that in order that this Department shall be of the greatest service to commerce and industry, it should be maintained on a non-regulatory basis."

Hoover elaborated on his ideas in a slim 1922 volume, *American Individualism*. There he acknowledged the possibility that trade associations and labor unions might produce "a new setting of tyranny." If U.S. government officials were "timorous mediocrities dominated by groups," then "we shall become a syndicalist nation on a gigantic scale." But he took comfort in "the vast multiplication of voluntary organizations for altruistic purposes," which offered "proof of the ferment of spirituality, service, and mutual responsibility."

American Individualism attracted considerable attention because certain passages departed markedly from the reactionary temper of the postwar era. Hoover struck an emphatically progressive chord in writing:

> We have long since abandoned the laissez-faire of the 18th Century—the notion that it is "every man for himself and the devil take the hindmost," . . . in part because we have learned that it is the hindmost who throw bricks at our social edifice, in part because we have learned that the foremost are not always the best nor the hindmost the worst. . . . We have also learned that fair division can only be obtained by certain restrictions on the strong and the dominant.

The government regulation that "began strongly three decades ago," he pointed out, was "proof that we have gone a long way toward the abandonment of the 'capitalism' of Adam Smith." In the one pellucid sentence in the book, Hoover said, "There are continents of human welfare of which we have penetrated only the coastal plain."

As in his orations, however, most of *American Individualism* offered nothing that could not be heard at a weekly Kiwanis luncheon. "Acts and ideas that lead to progress are born out of the womb of the individual mind, not out of the mind of the crowd," he argued. "The crowd only feels: it has no mind of its own which can plan. The crowd is credulous, it destroys, it consumes, it hates, and it dreams—but it never builds." In a sentence he italicized, he stated that, though every individual should be safeguarded equality of opportunity, "he . . . must stand up to the emery wheel of competition." Government oversight, he conceded, had been "highly beneficial," but it had also been guilty of "throttling . . . initiative," and he deplored the tendency to "go too far and stifle the reproductive use of capital." While, in his neither-this-nor-that fashion, Hoover warned against "the equal dangers . . . of reaction and radicalism," he aimed his sharpest arrows at the left. "The will-o'-the-wisp of all breeds of socialism," he maintained, "is that they contemplate a motivation of human animals by altruism alone." In rejoinder, he stressed that "for the next several generations we dare not abandon self-interest as a motive force to leadership and to production, lest we die."

It is hard to fathom why this jejune screed, little more than a pamphlet, has been taken seriously as a meaningful contribution to social theory. A man who had already convinced himself that "we now have equality of opportunity," Hoover never gave more than a glance at the actual life choices faced by a Mississippi sharecropper or an Ohio seamstress. He churned out synthetic sentiments ("non-essentials are the real fertilizers of the soil from which spring the finer flowers of life") and cloddish locutions such as "production of the total product."

Current Opinion likened his chunky style to the wooden verbiage of Grover Cleveland, and the *New York Times* not long before had written that Hoover's statements "read like introductions to something he is about to say. Yet there is around all of them an atmosphere of saying something definitely. He is not a man to be suspected of evading any question, and therefore the only possible conclusion is that when he says nothing he really sincerely believes that he has said something; that he is simply unable to be definite, positive, concrete, in discussing public questions, though he certainly thinks he is as definite as anybody." No matter. The publication of *American Individualism* magnified the impression that Herbert Hoover was more than an officeholder. He was a statesman.

Hoover's ascent to the peak of national prominence came not from a book, however, but from a fortuitous crisis: the worst natural disaster in the nation's history, the 1927 Mississippi River flood. After days of relentless rain, the collapse of mighty levees let loose immense torrents of brown water, creating an inland sea a thousand miles long and fifty miles wide. People and livestock were drowned in an instant. The debacle left countless families homeless, their occupations gone, and with no way to feed themselves. Finding shelter and sustenance for these regiments of displaced Americans was an awesome challenge, and President Coolidge, who would have preferred to shirk all responsibility, knew there was only one person who could assume that chore. Reluctantly, he appointed Secretary Hoover to coordinate rescue and relief in the Mississippi Valley.

With a confidence born of having made it through far worse devastation in the Great War, Hoover swiftly took command. He set up headquarters in Memphis on the Chickasaw Bluffs, high above the raging river, but he spent most of the next three months traversing the valley in a private Pullman car—moving ceaselessly from Cairo to New Orleans and back again, often sleeping on the train or a boat. In each of the ninety-one communities he stopped at, he preached the same sermon: "A couple of thousand refugees are coming. They've got to have accommodations. Huts. Watermains. Sewers. Streets. Dining-halls. Meals. Doctors. Everything. And you haven't got months to do it. You haven't got weeks. You've got hours. That's my train." In *Rising Tide*, his most rigorous critic, John M. Barry, acknowledged that Hoover "performed magnificently during the initial stages of the flood." He sparked a fundraising drive that brought in $17 million; gathered an armada of six hundred vessels; and put together 150 tent cities as havens for multitudes of evacuees.

Hoover, who as secretary of commerce had quietly integrated

the Census Bureau and established the post of adviser on black economic development, gave particular attention to the plight of African Americans. He asked the Red Cross to place more blacks on its payroll, and he demanded that it determine whether "colored people are being restrained in the camps against their will, . . . are being tagged for return to specific plantations, . . . [and] are being charged by Red Cross for food." When the NAACP exposed abuses, he authorized Robert Russa Moton, Booker T. Washington's successor as head of Tuskegee Institute, to investigate. Hoover's concern went far beyond these steps. He saw the crisis as nothing less than an opportunity to reconfigure southern society. With singular foresight, he proposed the subdivision of plantations into small homesteads that tenants, notably African Americans, could buy, with the program to be financed by a private resettlement corporation.

Unhappily, the Mississippi flood, which showed Hoover at his best, also revealed him at his worst. Hoover exploded when Moton reported that blacks were conscripted at gunpoint to labor on the levees; "were beaten by soldiers"; "that more than one wanton murder was committed by these soldiers"; and "that women were outraged by these soldiers." In Hoover's words, he "laid Dr. Moton out." He refused to believe the findings and insisted that Moton rewrite the document. Any revelation of brutal mistreatment of African Americans and of the shortcomings of the Red Cross would undermine his assumptions about the virtues of voluntarism, private charity, and local control. His vision of a multitude of homesteads in the Deep South came to nothing because it depended upon private capital he could not raise, and when African American leaders asked how dislocated black croppers were expected to get through the coming winter, he snubbed them.

Moreover, Hoover, in a manner that by now had become characteristic, distorted the nation's response to the Mississippi calamity and what it signified. The country had come through the ordeal, he asserted, almost entirely because of community improvisation. "I suppose I could have called in the whole of the Army," he remarked later. "But . . . all I had to do was to call in Main Street."

Never would he acknowledge that two out of every three dollars spent to cope with the flood came from government or that he had depended on federal agencies—from the Public Health Service to the Department of Agriculture to the National Guard—for essentials of his operation: sixty planes, hundreds of ships, field equipment, and tents to quarter the victims.

Hoover, though, emerged from the venture more than ever a celebrity. Once again, he had become a "czar," but this time empowered even to issue orders to the army and navy. During the disaster, governors seeking aid ignored the president of the United States and communicated with Hoover instead, and his name appeared in the press more often than Coolidge's. Most important, he had become the protagonist in a melodrama watched by millions. In a "reminiscent biography" published in 1928, Will Irwin wrote: "I, who have followed Hoover on his great European jobs, would like to leave him as I saw him one May morning of 1927—standing on the tottering Melville levee, his aeroplanes scouting overhead, his mosquito-fleet scurrying below, a group of prominent citizens about him listening to the wise, quick, terse directions which were bringing order out of chaos. It symbolizes the man, that scene—'The one tranquil among the raging floods,' the transmuter of altruistic emotion into benevolent action."

5

The Road to the White House

The Mississippi flood saga catapulted Hoover into the perch of front-runner for the 1928 Republican nomination. Though he had not once been a candidate for any office, he had no difficulty imagining himself in the White House. As early as 1922, the antagonistic Hiram Johnson had written, "Hoover has an ambition that o'erleaps itself. He is perfectly mad to be President." In 1926, a year before Coolidge surprised the country by announcing, somewhat cryptically, that he did not "choose to run" for another term, Hoover had hired a publicity agent. His service in the cabinet under two presidents fitted him with impressive qualifications, for, as one observer commented, Hoover had "traveled around a wider arc of the circle of federal governmental functions and opportunities than anyone else." Furthermore, he exuded self-confidence. "I felt, looking at him," remarked Sherwood Anderson in 1927, "that he had never known failure."

Hoover, though, encountered a number of impediments on the road toward nomination. His eligibility was questioned because he had not, in the period immediately prior to 1928, "been fourteen Years a Resident within the United States," as the Constitution stipulated, and the allegation that he was a British subject took on life when an English clerk revealed that Hoover was on the voting rolls in a London district. Though Anglophobes bridled at the thought of Hoover in the Oval Office, the most rabid opposition to him came from the Republican right. "Financial men," a publisher wrote Chief Justice William Howard Taft, "say that they have a grievance against Hoover, dating back to the food administration days." Taft himself later expressed fears that Hoover was a "dreamer" with "some rather grandiose views" who labored "much under the Progressive influence." When it became likely that Hoover was going to be the GOP's choice, stock prices fell. By then, however, the naysayers had run out of time. At the Republican convention in Kansas City, Hoover won the presidential nomination by an overwhelming margin on the first roll call.

Stanford's president, Ray Lyman Wilbur, came up with a unique way for his boon companion to be formally notified on August 11, 1928, of the nomination—not, as was traditionally done, in a staged encounter on the candidate's front porch, but in the university's huge football stadium. There, in an acceptance address delivered one day after his fifty-fourth birthday, Hoover said: "In no other land could a boy from a country village, without inheritance or influential friends, look forward with unbounded hope. My whole life has taught me what America means. I am indebted to my country beyond any human power to repay." Identifying himself with Harding and Coolidge, he made a rash promise. "Given a chance to go forward with the policies of the last eight years," he told the rally of seventy thousand supporters, "we shall soon with the help of God be in sight of the day when poverty will be banished from this nation."

Though Hoover was seeking office as nominee of a major political party, he did not want to be mistaken for a politician. He dreaded hitting the campaign trail. When he finally heeded the plea of advisers to make at least a few public appearances, he sputtered, "I'll not kiss any babies." Yet, while assuming this nonpolitical stance, he busied himself assiduously, supervising campaign minutiae and laboriously preparing his own speeches, a process that consumed a disproportionate number of days. When an assistant prodded him to speak more frequently, he replied, "I can make only so many speeches. . . . I write a speech as I build a bridge, step by step, and that takes time."

Hoover's champions portrayed his disdain for politics as a virtue, demonstrating that he was concerned only with the public weal. Earlier in the decade, during his third year as secretary of commerce, the *Chicago Daily News* had chimed:

> Who kept the Belgians' black bread buttered?
> Who fed the world when millions muttered?
> Who knows the needs of every nation?
> Who keeps the keys of conservation?
> Who fills the bins when mines aren't earning?
> Who keeps the home fires banked and burning?
> Who'll never win a presidential position?
> For he isn't a practical politician?
> Hoover—that's all!

Campaign biographers saw his ostensible indifference to politics as appropriate to a new age when the state would be managed by technicians—a prospect that might have been a bit scary save that Hoover also embodied nineteenth-century pioneer values. He was likened to Charles Lindbergh, the Lone Eagle who, in his 1927 solo flight across the Atlantic and in his autobiography *We*, blended evocation of cherished traits of individualism with reverence for modern technology. While holding tradition in high regard, Hoover's presidency, his adherents said, would usher in a "New Day."

Most Americans had become acquainted with Hoover in the Great War, and his supporters did all they could to keep those memories bright. "When hate and cruelty and stupidity stalked the world unchallenged" and "when choking yellow fumes of gas were blowing straight into the young, eager faces of thousands of boys," wrote the novelist Kathleen Norris, "there was a big, silent, efficient American man planted in Belgium fighting disease and starvation with American food, and fighting hate of the enemy with America's characteristic love for the suffering."

Recollections of his years of service and the vision of a New Era appealed especially to progressives, including the revered Jane Addams of Hull House. They were gratified when Hoover warned against excessive use of injunctions against labor unions; advocated public works to employ the jobless; and announced that he favored a shortened workday, more spending for education, and "hundreds of millions" of dollars to help the farmer. One progressive demurred, but only because he thought Hoover altogether too militant. "Mr. Hoover has always shown a most disquieting desire to investigate everything and to appoint commissions and send out statistical inquiries on every conceivable subject under Heaven," Franklin D. Roosevelt complained to an industrialist. "He has also shown in his own Department a most alarming desire to issue regulations and to tell businessmen generally how to conduct their affairs."

Progressives seeking clues as to what kind of president Hoover might be would have done well to have scrutinized him more carefully. When Harding contemplated freeing the Socialist leader Eugene V. Debs from prison, Hoover had told him he was making a mistake. Throughout this period, he expressed intense hostility to proposals for federal operation of the power dam and nitrate plants at Muscle Shoals in the Tennessee Valley. In 1924 he wrote Ray Lyman Wilbur how displeased he was that some members of the Stanford faculty were backing the presidential candidacy of Senator Robert La Follette on a Progressive ticket, adding that engineers and economists who looked favorably on public power development and other heresies were either "deliberately untruthful or . . . incompetent." He realized that Wilbur was hampered by "that well established form of blackmail on Universities called Academic Freedom." Nonetheless, he instructed him, "You don't have to promote and advance this type of people."

His liberal supporters might also have taken note of several of his remarks on the campaign trail. At a Madison Square Garden rally, Hoover, praising "the American system of rugged individualism," denounced "every step of bureaucratizing the business of our country." He accused his Democratic opponent, Governor Al Smith, a moderate who would later be a ferocious critic of the New Deal, of being a covert Socialist and expressed alarm that "the points of contact between the government and the people are constantly multiplying." To cater to southern whites, he denied that he opposed Jim Crow; allowed his subordinates to make racist remarks; and ignored an appeal to denounce the Ku Klux Klan. (The Democrats were far worse.) Hoover's behavior in these instances was not only discreditable, it was unnecessary. Heading the ticket of the majority party at a time of unparalleled prosperity, he enjoyed the further advantage of facing a rival who roiled certain sensibilities by being a Roman Catholic from New York's Lower East Side, a product of the Tammany Hall machine, and a foe of Prohibition.

Hoover had only one liability: he seemed to be a cold fish. Henry Pringle, the saucy biographer of Teddy Roosevelt, reported after a 1928 interview with Hoover:

> He rises awkwardly as a visitor is shown to his desk, and extends his hand only halfway, in a hesitant fashion. His clasp is less than crushing. Then he sits down and waits for questions. His answers are given in a rapid, terse manner and when he is finished he simply stops. Other men would look up, smile, or round off a phrase. Hoover is like a machine that has run down. Another question starts him off again. He stares at his shoes, and because he looks down so much of the time, the casual guest obtains only a hazy impression of his appearance.

He exuded a grouchy impatience. "You can't expect to see calves running in the field the day after you put the bull to the cows," Coolidge once admonished him. "No," Hoover replied, "but I would expect to see contented cows." It was a bright sally, but not even Coolidge, a legendary sourpuss, could abide Hoover's ill nature.

The country greatly admired Hoover but did not warm to him as it had to Teddy, or did later to FDR, Ike, and Reagan. The standard monograph on the 1928 campaign was to underscore the unlikeli-hood of Hoover's ever becoming a charismatic figure: "His hair parts in the middle and his Christian name is Herbert." Further-more, his face was "immobile," his movements "ponderous," and he favored a stiff high collar years out of fashion. Even when he went fly-fishing, he wore a double-breasted blue serge suit. H. L. Mencken labeled the chubby candidate—whose face, it was later said, had a "curiously lunar terrain"—a "fat Coolidge." In titling a 1928 maga-zine article, one writer found it necessary to pose the question "Is Hoover Human?" Hoover's stolid demeanor constituted a chal-lenge for his publicists, but one of his campaign biographers was up to it. Hoover's feeling for the downtrodden, Irwin wrote, "trans-lates itself not into tears but into action. 'What can I do?' he asks himself; and the mind once more takes control. Henceforth, while others weep, he works!" For many he was, despite his lack of mag-netism, heroic.

. . .

When his train pulled into the depot on election day, Hoover, who had arrived in Palo Alto a generation before a friendless stranger, found a crowd of ten thousand awaiting him and the Stanford band ready to escort him to the polling station. Overhead, from a circling plane, a pilot tossed out firecrackers that, on exploding, re-vealed the flags of every country on the globe. That night, Hoover chalked returns on a blackboard in his spacious living room. At 7:30 p.m. West Coast time, a United Press wire conveyed Governor Smith's concession. "He should have conceded three hours ago, or, better still, three months ago," Hoover responded.

The first person born west of the Mississippi to be elected presi-dent, Hoover had won a resounding victory. In a contest with a heightened turnout, he received 21.4 million votes to Smith's 15 million and ran up a 444–87 advantage in the electoral college, in-cluding four states from the "Solid South." Led by John Philip Sousa, two thousand jubilant students paraded up a hill to the home of the president-elect—the March King's seventy-piece band blaring forth "El Capitan" and "Stars and Stripes Forever" accompanied by booming cheers for Stanford's most famous alumnus.

To an unusual extent, commentators polarized in speculating about what the landslide portended. "Competent observers," reported the *Nation*, "say that Mr. Hoover's Administration will either be, on the purely executive side, one of the most memorable in our history, or that he will be one of the greatest failures in the Presidency." His admirers had no doubt about what his accession to the White House would bring. To the pugnacious labor leader John L. Lewis, Hoover was "the foremost industrial statesman of modern times." Even more striking was the expectation of a former muckraker who had become a gullible enthusiast for what was dubbed fondly *the Soviet experiment*. "Big business in America is producing what the Socialists held up as their goal: food, shelter, and clothing for all," stated Lincoln Steffens. "You will see it during the Hoover administration."

Others, though, including some who were close to Hoover, wondered whether he had the proper temperament. An engineer, he once said, could fashion a waterfall much more beautiful than nature ever had. His listeners were aghast. On another occasion, he ruminated about whether an earthquake or powerful winds might topple a skyscraper. The correspondent with whom he was discussing the subject later reflected: "What particularly struck me at the time was the cold engineering question which he puzzled over; the other results of such a catastrophe apparently did not concern him at all." Hoover boasted of establishing ideas on "a practical economic basis, more and more stripped of the purely emotional side." In 1928 he had remarked, "It has been no part of mine to build castles of the future but rather to measure the experiments, the actions, and the progress of men through the cold and uninspiring microscope of fact, statistics, and performance."

Even at the outset, some observers felt premonitory chills. "I don't think he can sublet the job of emotional appeal," the editor William Allen White remarked early in December. "There seems to be a broad feeling that he is too much a machine," a close associate

commented. Similarly, the *New York Times* questioned whether being "a glutton for statistics" obsessed with "the elimination of waste"
equipped a man to be national sovereign. "A technologist, he does not
discuss ultimate purposes," wrote *Time* during the 1928 campaign.
"In a society of temperate, industrious, unspectacular beavers, such
a beaver-man would make an ideal King-beaver. But humans are
different. People want Herbert Hoover to tell where, with his extraordinary abilities, he would lead them."

Some found Hoover's cast of mind troubling. His economic
conceptions, wrote the economist George Soule, were "conceived
in advance of the evidence, and . . . held stubbornly after the evidence goes against him." That remark anticipated the historian Alfred Rollins's subsequent judgment: "Hoover almost always went
deep with a problem, but the depth was like a mineshaft, straightly
walled by Hoover's presumptions. Though his views were always
well documented, they frequently lacked all understanding of the
complex human and social ramifications of the problem. At the
moment of their impact on history, Hoover's narrowness betrayed
him."

The *New Republic* thought it "a poor omen" that Republican
power brokers had so little liking for their own candidate. Their
"suppressed uneasiness and irritation justify the prediction of . . .
either a stormy or compromising career as President." Until now,
Hoover had survived by confining his engineering techniques to increasing the profits of industrialists, the periodical observed, but as
president he was going to have to tackle problems such as unemployment that would inevitably entail "a heavy cost." It concluded
with a prediction: "He will put up a valiant but probably in the end
an unsuccessful fight. The inertia of the Republican politicians
and the unintelligence of American businessmen in relation to public
affairs will wear him out. He will be unable to recruit the following
with which successfully to oppose them, and he will in the end either
conform or quit."

Nothing put Hoover at greater risk than the extravagant expectations his champions had aroused. "A vote for Herbert Hoover,"

Republican ads proclaimed, "is a vote for . . . the party that has wiped out soup-kitchens . . . and bread lines from the land"; campaign workers distributed copper Hoover Lucky Pocket Pieces inscribed "Good for four years of prosperity." In placing his name before the Republican convention, a Californian had characterized him as "engineer, practical scientist, minister of mercy to the hungry and the poor, administrator, executive, statesman, beneficent American, kindly neighbor, wholesome human being." Hoover "sweeps the horizon on every subject," he declared. The press often went even further, hailing him as "a genius" and as the "most useful American citizen now alive." George Washington had been a pretty good president, acknowledged the *Los Angeles Times*, but "he had never had the training or experience of Herbert Hoover."

These encomiums troubled no one more than the president-elect as he contemplated what the future had in store. In late January 1929, at the Florida vacation home of J. C. Penney on Biscayne Bay, he told the editor of the *Christian Science Monitor*: "I have no dread of the ordinary work of the presidency. What I do fear is the . . . exaggerated idea the people have conceived of me. They have a conviction that I am a sort of superman, that no problem is beyond my capacity. . . . If some unprecedented calamity should come upon the nation . . . I would be sacrificed to the unreasoning disappointment of a people who expected too much."

6

False Dawn

On March 4, 1929, Hoover took the oath of office as thirty-first president of the United States. America, its new leader told the rain-soaked crowd of fifty thousand at the Capitol and countless more listening on the radio, was "filled with millions of happy homes; blessed with comfort and opportunity." He spoke in a monotone, but his words were oracular. "We are steadily building a new race, a new civilization great in its own attainments," he claimed. "I have no fears for the future of the country," he declared. "It is bright with hope." One assertion, more than any other, heralded the theme of his inaugural address: "In no nation are the fruits of accomplishment more secure."

Through much of his term, critics would harpoon that sentence. Those words, they said, reflected the smug impudence of the New Era. Moreover, they went on, Hoover was—in the phrase of the day—asking for it. In 1932 a journalist, remarking on similar gasconades during the 1928 campaign, observed, "Never in American history did a candidate so recklessly walk out on a limb and challenge Nemesis to saw it off."

Most Americans, though, found Hoover's contention altogether reasonable. For years, they had seen the burgeoning manifestations of the consumer culture: Fords, Studebakers, and Pierce-Arrows; refrigerators, electric toasters, and rayon frocks; the surging stock market, soaring skyscrapers, and rising real wages. In 1929 unemployment bottomed at 3 percent. "The more or less unconscious and unplanned activities of business men," wrote Walter Lippmann, "are for once more novel, more daring, and in general more revolutionary than the theories of the progressives."

Hoover's entry into the White House lifted the Great Bull Market still higher. "Messages from virtually every city in the country, from Maine to California and from Washington State to Florida, have directed brokers in New York to buy stocks, indicating a conviction that the Hoover Administration is to inaugurate a period of unparalleled prosperity," the country's foremost Republican newspaper, New York's *Herald-Tribune*, reported. "Confidence in this prosperity, belief that times with Mr. Hoover at the helm will be even better than they are now has been manifest ever since the election. . . . There has been an almost unprecedented display of conviction on the part of the investing public that with Hoover at the throttle the signal is full steam ahead." By September, General Electric was trading at 396, three times what it had been in the spring of 1928.

"We were in a mood for magic," the *New York Times* correspondent Anne O'Hare McCormick wrote a year later. "Mr. Hoover was inaugurated, and the whole country was a vast, expectant gallery, its eyes focused on Washington. We had summoned a great engineer to solve our problems for us; now we sat back comfortably and confidently to watch the problems being solved. The modern technical mind was for the first time at the head of a government. . . . Almost with the air of giving genius its chance, we waited for the performance to begin."

Even before taking office, Hoover, in assembling his cabinet, had shown an instinct for command. He persuaded the distinguished patrician Henry Stimson, who had served as secretary of war and governor-general of the Philippines, to become secretary of state. When Andrew Mellon insisted on retaining his Treasury post, in good part because he thought that Hoover was, in the words of the financier's biographer, "a closet interventionist" who was not a true believer in the free market, Hoover, as best he could, bypassed him and relied instead upon the aluminum magnate's undersecretary, Ogden Mills. Hoover also felt free to name a Missouri car dealer secretary of agriculture, for he meant to till that field himself. He was particularly delighted that Ray Lyman Wilbur consented to be secretary of the interior, the department in which the president vested most of his hopes—for conservation, child welfare, public health, and a host of other activities.

Progressives, who were often discontent in the Harding-Coolidge period, had good cause to be pleased with Hoover's initial actions. During his first week in office, the president declared that "excessive fortunes are a menace to true liberty," and a few days later he insisted that the public be informed of government rebates of income, gift, and estate taxes, though he knew that Mellon strenuously opposed such disclosures. Hoover also ordered his attorney general to publish the names of all supporters of judicial appointments, so that special interests would be divulged.

During the 1928 campaign, Hoover had promised to call Congress into special session for prompt action on tariff revision and farm relief, and three days after he was sworn in he honored that pledge. He wanted only "limited changes in the tariff," but they included taking the power to set rates away from Congress and vesting it in a commission that could raise or lower duties "scientifically," with no regard to the demands of lobbyists. The object of his agricultural policies, he had explained in his inaugural address, was to give "our farmers an income equal to those of other occupations; . . . the farmer's wife the same comforts in her home as women in other groups; [and] . . . farm boys and girls the same opportunities in life as other boys and girls."

He had every reason to believe that the legislation would be swiftly approved. His party enjoyed an advantage of seventeen seats in the Senate, and more than one hundred in the House. The Speaker of the House, Nicholas Longworth, thought Congress would take no more than a month to give the president what he wanted. A week before Congress met on April 15, 1929, the *New York Times* declared,

"The skies appear clear blue for the Hoover administration. The indications are that harmony will be the rule." That same month, a maverick South Dakota senator wrote, "The President is so immensely popular over the country that the Republicans here are on their knees and the Democrats have their hats off."

Hoover benefited greatly from the goodwill he had engendered with the press during his years as secretary of commerce. "Long before the death of Harding, it became the custom of a group of correspondents, including some of the ablest in the business, to gather several afternoons each week in Hoover's office," remarked the well-regarded Washington reporter Paul Y. Anderson. "There he talked freely." As soon as Hoover became president, he delighted the press corps by announcing liberalization of the rules for quotation that had been imposed by Coolidge. "From every standpoint of frankness, honesty and practicality," Anderson stated, "the new system is a vast improvement."

The press gave him high marks for the way he pushed through agricultural legislation that spring. He beat back an attempt by the farm bloc to impose an export bounty and gained congressional approval for his own program. Instead of believing, as right-wingers did, that the federal government should not involve itself in local affairs, he favored massive intervention—but through loans, not grants—to enable farmers to create their own marketing alliances, like businessmen's trade associations. He wanted more farmers to have the advantages of cooperatives that butter marketers enjoyed with Land O'Lakes Creameries and orange growers with Sunkist. On June 15, exactly two months after Congress convened, Hoover signed into law the Agricultural Marketing Act of 1929, which set up a Federal Farm Board with a revolving fund of half a billion dollars to lend to farmer-owned co-ops. It also authorized stabilization corporations that could sustain farm income by buying crops, thereby keeping off the market temporary surpluses that would depress prices. "In many respects," wrote one rural journalist, "it is the most far-reaching bill presented to Congress since the Federal Reserve Act."

Throughout 1929 Hoover took a capacious view of his responsibilities in a manner gratifying to progressives. He backed the movement to establish a National Institute of Health, which Congress set up in 1930; sought reform of the jerry-built banking system; proposed braiding the spider's web of railway lines; and ordered the Census Bureau to determine the number of unemployed workers in the country. Asked by a business delegation for a favor, he responded, "Remember, gentlemen, when I was Secretary of Commerce I was devoting myself to your interests and now that I have become the leader of the nation, I must take the point of view of all people." He also showed the tolerance of dissent he had exhibited in 1919. If Communists picketed the White House, he instructed his attorney general, the government should do nothing to restrain them.

Almost always, Hoover launched programs not by drafting legislation but by putting together a commission or a conference. He established sixty-two fact-finding bodies and sponsored scores of gatherings, frequently paid for not by the government but by private philanthropy. "I only claim one distinction," said the humorist Will Rogers, "and that is that I am the only person that I know of that is not on one of his commissions."

The president's most ambitious commission emanated from a dinner at the White House in September 1929. The Research Committee on Social Trends enlisted some of the country's most eminent social scientists, including Charles Merriam of the University of Chicago, Wesley Mitchell of Columbia University, and Howard Odum of the University of North Carolina. Sidestepping Congress, Hoover financed it with a Rockefeller Foundation grant and took advantage of the facilities of the Social Science Research Council. He gave the group an enormous assignment—nothing less than a charge to survey the entirety of American society.

The commission eliciting the greatest press coverage arose in part from an event at a venue far removed from 1600 Pennsylvania Avenue: a Clark Street garage in Chicago where, in the St. Valentine's Day Massacre of 1929, Al Capone's thugs murdered six of

Bugs Moran's North Side hoodlums. In May Hoover—the first president to refer to crime in an inaugural address—established a National Commission on Law Observance and Enforcement under former U.S. attorney general George Wickersham. Its distinguished membership included Roscoe Pound, dean of Harvard Law School. The president asked the commission, while concentrating on Prohibition, to examine the rise in violence—especially the turf wars erupting in gangland over bootleg liquor. (Hoover also ordered the Department of Justice to move in on Capone, a project that led to the arrest and conviction of Scarface for tax evasion.)

The shocking findings of the Wickersham Commission had far-reaching reverberations. The *Report on Lawlessness in Law Enforcement* has been hailed as "one of the most important events in the history of American policing," and the *Report on the Causes of Crime* has been said to mark "the coming-of-age of American criminology." These documents awakened the country to the extent of brutal police practices, notoriously the third degree ("the inflicting of pain, physical or mental, to extract confessions or statements") and "cold storage" (holding the accused incommunicado for days). The commission also focused a harsh spotlight on other transgressions: fabrication of evidence, coercion of witnesses, entrapment, and bribery. Its recommendations for more systematic compilation of crime data and for better-trained officers who were not subservient to political machines sparked reforms in a number of cities.

A riot at Leavenworth penitentiary in 1929 punctuated the urgent need for a related Hoover program: penal reform. The president appointed the renowned commissioner of the Massachusetts Department of Corrections, Sanford Bates, to head a newly created Bureau of Prisons, which drafted eight pieces of legislation that Congress later enacted. A $5 billion appropriation made it possible for Bates to institute a school for prison guards, set up work camps, improve health care for inmates, and—in order to relieve overcrowding of penitentiaries—build new facilities, including escape-proof Alcatraz.

. . .

By mixing public and private institutions, Hoover nudged the country, however guardedly, toward an approximation of a welfare state.
He cajoled insurance company underwriters into writing old-age
pension policies as the first step toward a national system, and he
looked into the experience of other lands with unemployment insurance. To meet the needs of the millions of Americans who lived
in wretched dwellings, he convoked the nation's first housing conference. To care for the Great War's doughboys, as well as men—
some of them broken—who had returned from other wars, he issued
an executive order setting up a new agency: the Veterans Administration.

Less than four months after taking office, Hoover, who had written a "Child's Bill of Rights," called a White House Conference on
Health and the Protection of Children, which he financed with
leftover funds from wartime relief for Belgium. It drew well over
three thousand delegates to Washington and resulted in a thirty-five-
volume report that sparked state and local action. The conferees,
who found that six million American children were undernourished,
recommended abolishing child labor, creating public welfare services
for children in need, and instituting safeguards against neglect and
exploitation. Hoover also jacked up appropriations. "I would be
obliged," he told his budget director in the fall of 1929, "if you would
treat with as liberal a hand as possible the applications of . . . the
Children's and Women's Bureaus. I have great sympathy with the
tasks they are undertaking."

An avid outdoorsman, Hoover augmented the national forest
reserve by two million acres. He came to the rescue of sequoia groves
on the Pacific Coast, where Secretary Wilbur founded the "Save the
Redwoods League," and he issued an edict restricting the gunning
down of migratory birds. Nine days after taking office, Hoover announced that no more oil exploitation would be permitted on public lands, and, within the next year, more than twelve thousand

leases were canceled. But his most important step on behalf of conservation was approving as director of the National Park Service the superbly qualified Horace Albright, another Californian. Under Hoover and Albright, the government added three million acres to U.S. parks and monuments—a phenomenal 40 percent increase. It opened preserves in the Grand Tetons and Carlsbad Caverns, and took steps toward creating the first national parks in the East, including the Great Smokies and the Florida Everglades.

Instead of coping piecemeal with issues of water resources development, Hoover envisioned a comprehensive national program, including a grand network of inland waterways and power grids. To take advantage of the mighty river that the United States shares with Canada, he advocated constructing a St. Lawrence Seaway that would transform Midwestern commerce by opening Duluth, Chicago, and Toledo to oceangoing vessels, thus making them Atlantic ports. To rationalize the hydroelectric power system, he asked Congress to expand the Federal Power Commission's authority over interstate private utilities. In June 1929, thanks largely to Hoover's instigation, Congress approved the Boulder Canyon Project Act to generate more than three million kilowatt hours of hydroelectric power, curb floods in the Imperial Valley, and supply water to households in Southern California. The waters of the Colorado, the president declared, instead of "being wasted in the sea," would benefit "millions of happy homes . . . out under the blue sky of the West."

• • •

On some matters, Hoover's reputation for progressivism rests on developments that came to fruition not in his first months in office but later in his term. The Norris–La Guardia Act, which limited injunctions as strike-breaking weapons, did not win approval until 1932. It was not a product of the Great Depression but of a determined campaign by trade unions to shackle hostile judges. Businessmen, despairing of defeating the bill in Congress, looked to

Hoover to veto it. Instead, he signed it. This historic statute, Irving Bernstein has written, was "labor's greatest legislative victory" of this period and "a lone bright star in an otherwise dark sky."

Hoover delighted liberals, too, by his choice of a successor to the legendary Supreme Court justice Oliver Wendell Holmes Jr., who stepped down in 1932. The president came under considerable pressure to fill the vacancy with the distinguished jurist Benjamin Cardozo. For a time, he hesitated. No one could question the qualifications of the author of the classic *The Nature of the Judicial Process*, but appointing Cardozo would create a geographical imbalance, with three justices—one-third of the Court—from the state of New York. Furthermore, anti-Semites, who had savaged Louis Brandeis when Wilson nominated him in 1916, balked at giving a second place on the high bench to a Jew. But Hoover wound up submitting Cardozo's name. When the Senate approved, William Allen White wrote a leading progressive: "I have not had a good drink since I left Kansas City to come to Emporia nearly 40 years ago. . . . Hunt up . . . a good long brown drink of nose-choking, hair-raising, gullet-giggling hard corn liquor and . . . take one happy untrammeled drink for me in celebration of Justice Cardozo."

Before selecting Cardozo, Hoover had made two other appointments to the Supreme Court. The Senate took only one minute to whoop through Owen Roberts, prosecutor of the Teapot Dome miscreants, unanimously. But the president's choice of Charles Evans Hughes as chief justice engendered considerably more controversy, with twenty-six senators voting against confirmation of a man they distrusted as a corporate lawyer. Progressives, who failed to measure the extent of Roberts's conservatism, also did not perceive that Hughes was a committed civil libertarian; during Hoover's presidency, Chief Justice Hughes delivered two pathbreaking opinions expanding constitutional protection of freedom of expression.

Hoover also espoused policies that advanced the rights of ethnic groups. To redress the shabby record of the federal government toward Native Americans, he named as Indian commissioner Charles J. Rhoads, a former president of the Indian Rights Association—a choice John Collier, who was to head the "Indian New Deal," judged "well nigh incredibly fortunate." Rhoads speedily abolished segregated Indian boarding schools, and Hoover, overriding the objections of the budget director, increased appropriations for the Indian Bureau. The additional money permitted Rhoads to double the clothing allowance for Native American pupils and more than triple their food subsidy. He also built modern hospitals and hired better-trained doctors; under Hoover, trachoma among Indians was cut in half. Collier, a feisty critic, later said that the "real shift" toward acknowledging Indian rights began not with FDR but with Hoover.

Though flawed, Hoover's perception of African Americans did not embody the prejudices of his times. On buying a house in Washington, the Hoovers had refused to sign a restrictive covenant barring resale to Jews or African Americans, though such compacts were commonplace. The president not only supported the Urban League but made a sizable contribution to it. In addition, he increased appropriations for Howard University and nearly doubled those for the Freedmen's Hospital. He instructed his attorney general to make sure that the composition of a newly created Board of Parole reflected the percentage of African Americans and women in prisons; appointed an adviser to promote black economic development by the Department of Labor; and got the Rosenwald Fund to put up the money for a Conference on the Economic Status of the Negro.

None of these actions attracted nearly so much attention as a minor social event—veritably a tempest over a teapot. After almost all the congressional spouses had been entertained in large gatherings at the White House, Lou Hoover arranged an intimate tea in the Green Room for the wife of the newly elected Republican congressman from Illinois Oscar DePriest, who was black. Not since Theodore Roosevelt had provoked outrage from racists by dining with Booker T. Washington had there been an African American guest in the executive mansion. Three southern legislatures troubled to adopt resolutions reprimanding the First Lady, and a southern newspaper said that she had "defiled the White House." Fortunately, the president told his wife, "the world to come" had a "hot hell" reserved for such people.

Hoover won further approval from liberals for his conduct of foreign affairs, especially his single-minded pursuit of disarmament. In the summer of 1929, he appointed a commission to determine how to reduce military personnel, and he closed down naval construction projects. "Nothing could be a finer or more vivid conversion of swords to plowshares," he declared, than downsizing the U.S. Navy. "Levels of naval strength," he reaffirmed in his Armistice Day address, "could not be too low."

In this campaign, Hoover found an ardent accomplice in Britain's new Labour prime minister, the pacifist J. Ramsay MacDonald, who sailed to America to explore how to downsize navies. He met with the president at secluded Rapidan Camp, precisely one hundred miles from the White House—a rustic retreat by a trout stream deep in the Blue Ridge Mountains of Virginia where Hoover could escape "the pneumatic hammer of public life." On a sparkling Sabbath morning in October 1929, the autumn woods scarlet with sumac, the president and the prime minister talked amiably seated on a log by a cascade. Journalists rated Hoover's Rapidan meeting, which elicited a florescence of Anglo-American goodwill, a "diplomatic triumph." No newspaper was more viscerally critical of Republicans than the country's foremost Democratic organ, the *World* of New York. But the *World* called Hoover's performance in foreign affairs over his first eight months "dazzling." When the president attended a World Series game in Philadelphia in October, the crowd at Shibe Park responded to "Hail to the Chief" by giving him a standing ovation.

• • •

This impressive record, most of it compiled during his first year in office, has led a number of commentators—both contemporaries and historians—to contend that, if he had not had the undeserved misfortune of the Great Depression, Herbert Hoover would have been rated in the upper ranks of American presidents. As early as

1935, his former press secretary wrote of Hoover: "He had planned many changes for the betterment of government. . . . He would have forwarded many more changes if conditions had been normal—and strange as it may seem, he would have gone down in history as a moderately liberal President." In an obituary in 1964, the London *Times* said of Hoover: "He will be remembered as one of the unluckiest men ever to be elected President of the United States. Had he held office at a time of normal strain his rule would probably have been noted for quiet success and smooth progress." Similarly, David Burner has written that Hoover's "early tenure was a remarkable experiment in developing new approaches," and the historian Robert Sobel has concluded, "Without the depression, Hoover would have gone on to a second term and retired in triumph in 1937."

Even at the time, however, analysts questioned such judgments. Hoover had trouble with the legislative branch almost from the beginning, much of it his own making. During consideration of the farm bill—his one legislative accomplishment in 1929—he was curiously torpid. At a breakfast meeting with congressional leaders in the White House, he offered nothing. The rest of that first session was a bust. The president believed his plan for "limited revision" of the tariff to benefit farmers would be quickly enacted, but, as anyone less naive than Hoover about Capitol Hill could have predicted, it immediately fell prey to avaricious lobbies. Repelled by logrolling, Hoover made no attempt to use his influence to fashion an acceptable bill. Well before the Wall Street crash, Hoover had been exposed as politically inept and incapable of mobilizing his own party.

On reconvening, Congress took up the tariff issue once more—again without guidance from Hoover. "When the high-tariff wolves took charge of the bill and began writing outrageous new duties into it, he said nothing to rebuke them," wrote the journalist and historian Allan Nevins. "His handling of the whole situation showed an astonishing clumsiness." During the wrangling, the Senate came within one vote of restricting the revision of schedules to agriculture, but Hoover did not lift a finger. The Hawley-Smoot bill raised the tariff to the highest level in the twentieth century, with rates hiked on 887 items. Hoover's lassitude severed his ties to the progressive wing of his party. His closest adviser in the Senate, William Borah, cut him off, and Senator Smith Wildman Brookhart of Iowa offered a public apology for the hundreds of campaign speeches he had given on Hoover's behalf.

More than a thousand economists beseeched the president not to sign the bill, which was also disapproved by much of the Republican press and the American Bankers Association. Thomas Lamont of the House of Morgan later said: "I almost went down on my knees to beg Herbert Hoover to veto the asinine Hawley-Smoot Tariff. That Act intensified nationalism all over the world." Secretary of State Stimson warned that the legislation would disrupt the international financial community, and Hoover's correspondence secretary, after perusing mail to the White House, informed the president that "there has seldom been in this country such a rising tide of protest as has been aroused by the tariff bill."

Nonetheless, on June 17, 1930, Hoover signed the measure with a flourish—using six gold pens. Having earlier deluded himself that "the protective principle" was "the largest encouragement to foreign trade," he now denied that Hawley-Smoot raised rates. Though he purported to be a man who would heed the counsel of experts, he chose to ignore it, making himself the target for blame when Hawley-Smoot provoked economic retaliation by other countries or offered a plausible rationale for it. "In France," a leading economist pointed out, "our tariff was compared to a declaration of war, an economic blockade." Hoover's friendly biographer Harris Warren summed up this "political disaster" by writing that "probably nothing was so damaging to Hoover's reputation during his first two years in the presidency as his handling of the tariff."

Hoover did not conceal his contempt for members of Congress. One U.S. senator, he said, was "the only verified case of a negative I.Q." After conferring with the president about senators, Secretary

Stimson noted that "he had bad impressions about every one of them," though some were Hoover loyalists. The president told a member of the Federal Reserve Board that he "had no idea how I had to demean myself before those Democratic swine" and referred to Congress as "that beer garden up there on the hill." At the Gridiron Club dinner in 1930, he made a remark that was unlikely to improve relations with Congress: "It is an extraordinary thing . . . that the whole nation should shudder with apprehension and fear of an extra session of its great legislative body." As one contemporary said of Hoover: "He has never really recognized the House and Senate as desirable factors in our government."

Increasingly, he could not even get on with members of his own party. In May 1930 a powerful North Carolina congressman stated that Hoover was "so unpopular that each and every Republican Member seems to be going his own way," and the columnist Frank R. Kent, who was regarded as one of Hoover's coterie of pet journalists, thought him "the most left-footed President politically the world ever saw." Little more than a year after Hoover took office, the *New York Times* wrote of the Seventy-first Congress: "The session, which actually began with the Republican party united and expressing extreme friendliness to the administration, quickly became critical. . . . As it progressed, Republicans vehemently attacked the President because of his refusal to state his views on the tariff bill and for many months this hostility has been manifest." On Capitol Hill, a Republican senator regaled his colleagues with the tale that kidnappers had seized the president, leaving a ransom note warning that if they were not paid half a million dollars, they would return him to the White House.

Unlike a Teddy Roosevelt or a Woodrow Wilson, Hoover refused to go to the people to bring pressure on Congress, and he balked at using patronage as an enticement because he thought such activity was demeaning. "Politics is one of the minor branches of harlotry," commented William Allen White, "and Hoover's frigid desire to live a virtuous life . . . is one of the things that has reduced the oil in his machinery and shot a bearing." The president paid a high price for his aloofness. His "decision in favor of a more passive role," the political scientist Lawrence Chamberlain later concluded, "deprived him of an opportunity to establish his leadership at the very outset of what proved to be an unhappy administration."

The one important piece of legislation that Hoover did put through in 1929 came to grief in good part because he subverted its announced intention: empowering farmers to control their own destiny. He picked to head the Federal Farm Board not a man of the soil but a corporation mogul: the president of International Harvester, the big agricultural implements manufacturer many farmers regarded as their enemy. The other board members came from similar backgrounds. Hoover's appointees, Senator Norris said, "have grown, and grown fat, have become millionaires, all from the money they have received from the farmers of America." In addition, the president instructed the board to define its sphere narrowly. Though the act authorized stabilization operations, he did not want the board to pursue them. "Even indirect purchase and sale of commodities," he emphasized, were "absolutely opposed to my theory of government."

A number of Hoover's other initiatives miscarried too. When a problem arose requiring decisive action, his penchant for appointing a commission often resulted in delay and muddle. Little came of the ambitious agenda of the conferences he mustered, especially when the delegates sought increased federal responsibility. Unwilling to energize the national government to make sure that those who needed housing were provided for, Hoover got nothing of significance from the builders in whom he placed his trust. Instead of regarding the dire findings of his conference on child welfare as requiring a federal salvo, he sugarcoated them. When conferees expressed alarm that 10 million American children were impoverished or physically handicapped, he retorted: "Let us bear in mind that there are 35,000,000 reasonably normal, cheerful human electrons radiating joy and mischief and hope and faith. Their faces are turned toward the light—theirs is the life of great adventure. . . . We have a right to assume that we have a larger proportion of happy, normal children than any other country in the world."

With no input from Hoover, the Research Committee on Social Trends produced results falling far short of the lofty expectations of September 1929. The committee's 1,600-page report, *Recent Social Trends in the United States*, continues to be mined by scholars, but it had negligible impact on policy. The project was based on the conviction, as the historian Charles Beard later said, that "when once the 'data' have been assembled important conclusions will flow from observing them—conclusions akin in inevitability to those of physics or mathematics." The trouble with that notion is that "the scientific method is only a method. Dreams, plans, purposes, and collective will must come from the human mind and heart," Beard noted. "Hoover eventually disowned the study he so confidently commissioned on that Indian summer evening," David Kennedy has written. "A massive dreadnought of scholarship, its pages barnacled with footnotes, it was launched at last in 1933 onto a Sargasso Sea of presidential and public indifference."

The Wickersham Commission, while making a number of useful contributions, bungled its main assignment—what to do about Prohibition. Having underscored the deleterious impact dry laws were having on society, including ties of the illicit liquor trade to murderous gangsters, the commission appeared to be left with no choice save to recommend repeal of the Eighteenth Amendment. Instead, though only two of the eleven members thought that Prohibition was working well, it concluded that enforcement should continue. The document, said a New York congressman, was "Wicked-and-Sham."

Since, in Hoover's words, "the findings are wet and the recommendations are dry," the report became a laughingstock. The columnist Franklin P. Adams satirized its reasoning in doggerel:

> Prohibition is an awful flop.
> We like it.
> It can't stop what it's meant to stop.
> We like it.
> It's left a trail of graft and slime,
> It don't prohibit worth a dime,
> It's filled our land with vice and crime.
> Nevertheless, we're for it.

With adversaries more interested in the quarrel over booze than in his social and economic programs, Hoover, it was said, regarded both drys and wets as "substantially insane," but he could not free himself from the commitments he had made to drys in the 1928 campaign. Moreover, Hoover, whose mother had been a temperance crusader, had some sympathy for the Eighteenth Amendment because it demonstrated that "property rights did not dominate American ideals." Often misquoted as saying that Prohibition was "noble," he actually said, more circumspectly, that it was "a great social and economic experiment noble in motive and far-reaching in purpose." By misrepresenting the commission's findings and allying himself with zealots, however, he cast doubt on his credibility and permitted the columnist Heywood Broun to write: "Mr. Hoover stands revealed as the driest body this side of the Sahara. . . . He is for the Methodist Board of Morals lock, stock and bootlegger's barrels."

Hoover's conservation policies revealed a similar disharmony. When in October 1929 he created a Commission on the Conservation and Administration of the Public Domain, he stacked it with Republicans who shared his conviction that the federal government should relinquish unreserved public lands and new reclamation projects, even though vesting control in the states would leave the national heritage vulnerable to special interests. "Well," responded one newspaper, "conservation was a pretty dream while it lasted." Unexpectedly, however, the president and his commissioners were thwarted. Determined to "reduce Federal interference in affairs of essentially local interest," Hoover was taken aback when western states made clear that they did not want to be burdened by managing grazing lands, preferring instead to have Washington bureaucrats retain responsibility. Never able to understand why the states spurned this "gorgeous gift," Hoover, Kendrick Clements has commented, was "blinded" by the "triumph of ideological commitment over rationality."

The president had no more success in coping with the critical problem of overproduction of oil. "Hoover's policies were marked by a negation of leadership, by weakness and vacillation, by an unwillingness to confront prevailing problems, and by lack of realism and reluctance to experiment," the historian Gerald Nash has written. Hoover bought into the notion that at issue was "conservation" of resources, though a dissenter countered, "All this cant about conservation of oil for posterity is pure Bunk"; oil barons "care about as much for the welfare of posterity as the Devil does for the Trinity." The president reiterated his faith in private enterprise and states' rights even when industrialists raised an urgent cry for federal intervention. "Hoover showed himself to be singularly inept in his conduct of national petroleum policy," Nash concluded. "His lack of realism in approaching the industry's difficulties was extraordinary and compared most unfavorably with the insight of Harding and Coolidge."

In a number of ways, White House policies on water resources also disappointed conservationists. Hoover's plan for a national river system came to naught. The St. Lawrence Seaway treaty negotiated with Canada stalled in the U.S. Senate; not until 1959 was the project completed. Despite a clause in the Hoover Dam act giving preference to municipalities and other public bodies in the distribution of power, the administration favored private firms. To head the Federal Power Commission, Hoover chose a former attorney for the Alabama Power Company, and the FPC revealed its bias by firing employees who exposed unconscionable influence peddling.

Hoover's most important action on multipurpose river valley

development came in 1931 when Congress passed Senator Norris's bill for federal operation of the power site at Muscle Shoals, Alabama, and the measure reached his desk for signature. The legislation, the president said, must be judged by "the cold examination of engineering facts." Not facts, though, but ideology prevailed, for Hoover was outraged by the thought that the government would compete with privately owned utilities. "I hesitate to contemplate the future of our institutions, our government, and of our country if the preoccupation of its officials is to be no longer the promotion of justice and equal opportunity but is to be devoted to barter in the markets," he said in a contemptuous veto message. "This is not liberalism, it is degeneration." It fell to Franklin Roosevelt to seize the opportunity to make Muscle Shoals the keystone of his Tennessee Valley Authority, what the historian Sir Denis Brogan was to call "the dazzling TVA."

• • •

Out of this set of experiences, progressives came to believe that they had been hoodwinked—fools ever to think of Hoover as an enlightened statesman—and they reconsidered their assessment of his record on civil liberties, labor unions, and the treatment of racial minorities. Hoover, they noted, did not deter his secretary of labor, William Doak, from hunting aliens and deporting them. When their country of origin refused to accept them, the American government held them incommunicado for as long as a year and a half. Hoover signed the Norris–La Guardia anti-injunction bill, liberals maintained, only because he knew that, if he vetoed it, he would be overridden by embarrassingly huge margins. Furthermore, he accompanied his approval with an opinion by his attorney general all but inviting the U.S. Supreme Court to invalidate the law. The administration's policy toward Indians, so promising at first, did not bear scrutiny either. Ignoring all of the evidence of damage that assimilationists had done in snuffing out native culture, Secretary Wilbur insisted, "The redman's civilization must be replaced by the white man's."

Hoover pursued a southern strategy so feckless and so perverse that it loosened the traditional ties of African Americans to the Republicans, the party of the Great Emancipator. No amount of contrary evidence could dissuade him from the illusion that blacks in the South should trust their future to local white elites. In a highly sympathetic book, the historian Donald Lisio has stated that, whatever his intentions, the president's "venture into southern politics proved a sad encounter both for him and black Americans." He refused to issue even a ritualistic denunciation of lynching, and, in appointing a commission to explore home rule for Haiti, did not select a single African American. When Congress made it possible for Gold Star Mothers to make a pilgrimage to Europe, the secretary of war divided the women by race, and Hoover did not intercede to reverse the order. White mothers sailed to Europe in style, while black mothers whose sons had been killed in their country's service were assigned to "cattle ships." Hoover, asserted Walter White, executive director of the NAACP, was "the man in the lily-White House."

The president's nomination of John J. Parker to the U.S. Supreme Court in March 1930 compounded his difficulties. African Americans were incensed by the selection of a man who had once said that voting by Negroes was "a source of evil and danger," and who even in 1930 did not disown that statement. Parker had also infuriated organized labor by validating a sweeping injunction. The NAACP and union leaders set out to kill the nomination, and they did a better job than Hoover of mobilizing support. Hiram Johnson expected defeat "because our Ethiopian brethren are so aroused," and seventeen Republican senators, including the majority leader, urged Hoover to withdraw Parker's name. But the president insisted that he had better political intelligence and that his choice would be approved. In May the Senate rejected the nomination, with a good number of Republicans deserting Hoover. It was the first defeat of a president's nomination to the U.S. Supreme Court in more than a third of a century. Although Parker subsequently justified Hoover's confidence in him by distinguished service on a U.S. circuit court, the president had further alienated

African Americans and had again revealed to the country that he was a failed party leader.

Hoover, who had been a dynamo in Belgium as food czar and in the Mississippi Valley, seemed a considerably lesser presence in the Oval Office. In her fair-minded assessment of his first year as president, Anne O'Hare McCormick wrote: "President Hoover's procedure so far is that of the administrator rather than the executive, of the technical advisor rather than of the leader. There is hardly a single instance in which he has come out boldly for his own ideas, rallied the people in support of a cause, or given any indication that he considers such crusading the function of the Chief Magistrate." Hoover appeared to be congenitally incapable of demonstrating that he was caring—or willfully indifferent to the need to do so. The small departures he did introduce—as when he set up a new agency for veterans—he interred in deadening prose. Instead of speaking to the plight of maimed men condemned to spending the rest of their lives in hospital wards, he talked of achieving "important economies . . . in administration of . . . domiciliary questions."

His reputation diminished by so many setbacks, Hoover needed all the approval from the press he could muster, but he had long since squandered the goodwill that had been bestowed on him. Reporters became disillusioned when he demanded that they submit questions in writing a day in advance but ignored so many of their inquiries that they no longer bothered to raise them. Nonetheless, he wanted their stories turned in to him before they were published for "clearance." By the end of 1929, journalists were grumbling that they were getting less information from Hoover than they had from "Silent Cal." Since Hoover refused to say anything beyond what was in handouts, the devoted assemblage of two hundred correspondents with which he had started out dwindled to barely a dozen.

As the weeks went by, the attitude of the press corps moved from exasperation to animosity. "Except for a few favorites who cling to the White House," said one correspondent, "Mr. Hoover has scarcely a friend or defender among the hundreds of working news-paper men of Washington." By 1931 Paul Y. Anderson, who had initially been so pleased with the president's comportment, was writing that Hoover's relations with the press had descended to "a stage of unpleasantness without parallel in the present century . . . characterized by mutual dislike, unconcealed suspicion, and down-right bitterness." In August 1931 Hoover's press secretary, Theodore Joslin, noted in his diary, "The press is giving the president grave concern. Many of the men are hostile; not only the Democratic but the Republican writers." Hoover became so enraged at reporters that in 1932 he told Joslin: "Once I am re-elected I am going to clean that bunch out. . . . I have enough on fifty of them to hang them. Let any of them make one move after November and I'll go for them."

• • •

Is it conceivable that Hoover, despite these many tribulations, would have redeemed himself had he not been burdened by the al-batross of the Great Depression? Unlikely. "To say that he is a vic-tim of the panic and the depression, that if his outlook for victory is dark it is because he has hard luck, is in large part a misstate-ment," Allan Nevins observed in the summer of 1932. Not a cap-tious progressive but a writer soon to be the adulatory biographer of John D. Rockefeller, Nevins added: "The great initial loss of con-fidence in him occurred because at the outset, when the skies were brightest, he showed inability to lead; because he botched the tar-iff, he botched farm relief, he botched prohibition—because he showed a Bourbon temper and an inelastic mind. If there had been no panic or depression, he would have lost public support and de-served to lose it." A generation later, another historian agreed. "Even without the onset of the Great Depression," Gerald Nash observed, "it is doubtful whether Hoover would have succeeded . . . in imple-menting his programs."

One needs to bear in mind, though, the wide terrain to promote his ideas that an unimpeded four years would have given him.

Furthermore, in an age when Republicans were the majority party, there was every reason to suppose that Hoover would be reelected in 1932 and enjoy an eight-year run. But that was not to happen. "Instead of being able to devote my four years wholly to these programs," Hoover wrote in his *Memoirs*, "I was to be overtaken by the economic hurricane." It would not be the programs of his inaugural year but how he coped in the eye of the hurricane that would determine his place in history.

7

Crash

On Thursday, October 24, 1929, the New York Stock Exchange opened quietly, but volume was heavy and soon prices began to plunge at such a pace that the ticker could not keep up. "By eleven o'clock," John Kenneth Galbraith wrote later, "the market had degenerated into a wild, mad scramble to sell. By eleven-thirty the market had surrendered to blind, relentless fear." October 29, "Black Tuesday," was far worse: $30 billion in securities self-destructed. The next morning, the *New York Times* reported: "Stock prices virtually collapsed yesterday, swept downward with gigantic losses in the most disastrous trading day in the stock market's history." By mid-November, industrials were worth only half of what they had commanded ten weeks before. (Before Hoover left office, blue chip U.S. Steel dropped from 262 to 21, General Motors from 92 to 8, Montgomery Ward from 138 to 4.)

A number of Hoover's predecessors had confronted financial crises, but none had left him a usable legacy. In previous depressions—from 1837 to 1894—Martin Van Buren, James Buchanan, and Ulysses S. Grant had done nothing, and Grover Cleveland had taken a hard line against aid to the unfortunate. "All communities are apt to look to government for too much," Van Buren had declared, in explaining why he was going to "refrain from suggesting to Congress any specific plan for . . . relieving mercantile embarrassments." In later years, Hoover, too, would be categorized as a "do-nothing" president. In fact, as might have been expected of a man who had been so activist a secretary of commerce, he moved with commendable alacrity to arrest the decline.

Over nine days, starting in mid-November, the president summoned to the White House leaders of industry, finance, construction, public utilities, agriculture, labor, and the Federal Reserve system. A financial journalist opened his account of the gatherings by writing: " 'Order up the Moors!' was Marshal Foch's reply at the first battle of the Marne. 'Order up the business reserves' directed President Hoover as pessimistic reports flowed in from all quarters following the stock market crash." At this Conference for Continued Industrial Progress, as Hoover designated the meetings, he implored manufacturers to maintain wage rates—a policy, he believed, that would not only benefit workers but bolster the economy by sustaining consumer purchasing power. He asked unions to pledge not to strike and to withdraw pending demands for wage increases.

The president accompanied these pleas with reassurances. To calm nerves, he eschewed the familiar usage "panic" and instead designated the downturn a "depression," an unfortunate choice that would be forever associated with him. "The fundamental business of the country, that is production and distribution of commodities, is on a sound and prosperous basis," he declared. "Any lack of confidence in the economic future . . . in the United States is foolish." Critics soon were throwing these words back at him and charging him with irresponsible chatter, but it was perfectly reasonable for a chief executive to rally the nation. Hoover's assertions differed little from FDR's later contention that there was nothing to fear but fear itself.

Initially, Hoover succeeded beyond all expectations. Management and labor readily fell into line. The U.S. Chamber of Commerce created a National Business Survey Conference that drew upon the knowledge of some 170 trade associations. Henry Ford announced, as he emerged from the White House, that he was not only willing to adhere to the president's standard but actually going to raise wages. Hoover persuaded railroad executives to step up maintenance projects, and the head of the National Electric Light Association pledged to spend more than $100 million beyond the large sum it had invested in 1929. So euphoric was the mood Hoover generated that the Sears, Roebuck titan Julius Rosenwald expressed concern that the country might soon face a labor shortage. On December 5 Hoover reported to four hundred "key men" what he had accomplished at the November meetings. "The very fact that you gentlemen come together for these broad purposes," he told them, "is a far cry from the dog-eat-dog attitude of the business world of some thirty or forty years ago." The collaboration, Walter Lippmann wrote, "was an open conspiracy not to deflate."

The president took a number of other initiatives. He wired governors to encourage states and counties to accelerate construction. He urged Congress to appropriate $150 million for public works and to approve a tax cut. He coaxed the Federal Reserve Board to expand the money supply and to make more credit available; for the first time in the history of the republic, discount rates fell to under 2 percent. He counted on the Federal Farm Board to sustain crop prices, and for months the board did remarkably well, holding the price of U.S. wheat twenty-five cents or more a bushel above that in Europe. America now realized, said the *Boston Globe*, borrowing a phrase from Lippmann, "that it has at the White House a man who believes not in the philosophy of drift, but in the dynamics of mastery."

Despite all the rockets being fired from the White House, though, Hoover intended to limit the role of government. The amount he requested from Congress for construction was modest, and he advised governors that the "pursuit of public works" by the states should be "energetic yet prudent." Virtually all of the responsibility for the economic health of the nation was left with corporation directors. It was not clear, however, how much leadership would come from the private sector. The National Business Survey Conference contented itself with actions such as recommending that home owners spark revival by adding on "the extra sunporch." Moreover, if the system was "fundamentally sound," there was no need to inquire why the crash had happened or whether reforms might be required.

Hoover believed that the country was going through a short-term recession much like that of 1921, and hence drastic remedies were not required. Businesses continued to report year-end profits; the stock market gained several points; and, in contrast to past panics, no large bank or corporation had collapsed. Hoover has been roundly criticized for not realizing that the stock market crash signaled the onset of the Great Depression, but no one else—including liberals—had any more perception that the slump would last over a decade. At the end of 1929, the *New York Times* judged the most important news story of the year to be not the Wall Street blowup but Admiral Richard Byrd's expedition to the South Pole. The American Economic Association foresaw a brief downturn that could be beneficial. In 1930 the former chief of the War Industries Board, Bernard Baruch, a Democrat who was regarded as a financial wizard, foresaw that Hoover would be "fortunate enough, before the next election, to have a rising tide and then . . . will be pictured as the great master mind who led his country out of its economic misery."

Yet even before 1929 ended, cabinet officials were expressing concern about mounting unemployment, and by the spring of 1930 breadlines were familiar sights on city sidewalks. With municipal lodging houses bursting, New York put the homeless on a barge at an East River pier so that they would have a place to sleep. In midtown Manhattan on "one gusty March day in 1930," the historian Edward Robb Ellis has written, "hungry men stood in a triple line with their backs to the wind like cattle facing away from a storm," inching toward a soup kitchen in an Episcopal church. Of the two thousand shuffling in the cold, five hundred would be turned away when food ran out. That same month, Hoover claimed that "employment has been steadily increasing." In April, after the Census Bureau reported more than three million out of work (the figure was actually closer to four million), he shaved the total to below two million, which, he said, was normal.

Hoover never declared that prosperity was "just around the corner" (that fatuous statement came from the vice president, Charles Curtis), but he did refuse to face reality. In May 1930 he announced that a "great economic experiment" had "succeeded to a remarkable degree." He told the U.S. Chamber of Commerce, "We have passed the worst, and with continued effort we shall rapidly recover." When in June a delegation that included bankers as well as bishops arrived at the White House to alert him to the accelerating decline, Hoover, visibly annoyed, told them that the economy was on the upswing and the ranks of the unemployed were dwindling. "Gentlemen," he said, "you have come sixty days too late. The depression is over."

Disappointment in the president deepened. "By the rough judgments of politics," wrote Lippmann, "Mr. Hoover finds himself set down as an irresolute and easily frightened man." In July his public relations man in the 1928 campaign wrote him bluntly: "If you were running in New York today, I am sure . . . you could not carry the election. The public, . . . without regard to party, thinks the administration to date has been a failure." Later that season, the Canadian chargé d'affaires in Washington reported to Ottawa that Hoover was being "harassed and oppressed by difficulties the nature of which he is unfitted by his training and character to comprehend." Even Hoover's business allies found fault with him. New York's archconservative *Commercial and Financial Chronicle* concluded:

The brilliant conferences held in Washington last fall did a little good, no doubt, but only a little. They did not prevent unemployment, which increased almost steadily thereafter. They did not stabilize the prices of commodities, which have fallen since. They did not increase building operations beyond the appropriations for public buildings and roads. . . . They did not keep up the price of wheat, which is now . . . at exceedingly low levels. They did not prevent a recurrence of stock smashes, for at least one other of large dimensions has occurred since.

. . .

For Hoover, troubles never descended singly, but in twos and threes. That summer, at the same time muted factory whistles were testing his mettle, a devastating drought of historic proportions seared much of the heartland. A Red Cross investigator reported on conditions in eastern Arkansas: "Barefoot and without decent clothes, no meal, no flour in the bin, ragged children crying from hunger . . . nothing but . . . misery . . . far worse than the Mississippi flood." As in 1927, Hoover galvanized local communities and turned to the Red Cross, though he believed that reports of suffering were grossly exaggerated. So, too, did the Red Cross, which, thinking that starving supplicants were fakers, refused to spend much of the meager fund it had.

State authorities placed the need in the range of $120 million (almost certainly an underestimate), but the Hoover administration lowered the sum for federal aid to $25 million and specified that none of it could go for food. An Arkansas congressman wanted to know why the national government "would feed Jackasses but wouldn't feed starving babies." Many found it strange that a man who had made his reputation as an almoner in the Volga region not many years before would scruple about providing for his fellow citizens. Hoover, said Senator Tom Connally of Texas, had asked Congress for millions to feed "hungry Bolsheviks . . . with long whiskers and wild ideas," but now denied sustenance to hungry Americans.

Hoover's policies toward distress—in the drought-stricken counties and across the nation—reflected an aversion to the omnipotent state and a belief in "local government responsibilities." Even more important was the tradition of private giving. Grants from Washington, he contended, would impair the character of recipients and would deny benefactors the opportunity to sacrifice. The poor,

Hoover contended, could always count on their neighbors. Curiously, he was convinced that federal relief would debauch the poor, but handouts from private agencies or from local politicians would not. Hoover's hostility to federal intervention, William Allen White concluded, derived from "his passionate, almost bigoted, belief in America."

As the days dragged on, the inadequacy of this approach became more apparent. By autumn, cities were staggering under mounting job losses, and the countryside was devastated. At street corners across America men on the ragged edge set up stands to sell apples to passersby. New York City alone had six thousand vendors. Letters from desperate women to "Kind Mrs. Hoover," "Dear First Lady of the Land," or "Most Excellent Lady" told her, "Winter soon will be here and we just about barefooted no work can we find we do not have enough to eat you all have a plenty," or "Just a line to let you know i am a poor girl and i want to go to school and i ain't got the closes. . . . will you please send me some you old closes and thing you don't want?"

Hoover, though, had small patience with appeals to set off on a different path. When the president of General Electric urged him to call a special session of Congress to "request it to issue a billion dollars of bonds . . . to allay the tragic circumstances of unemployment," Hoover was incensed. Some time later, he received an accurate accounting of why federal relief was imperative: "Communities are impotent; state governments are shot through with politics . . . ; local charities are jaded, discouraged, bankrupt, disorganized, discredited. Their task is too great. Their support is gone." Hoover could barely contain himself in drafting a response: "This nation did not grow great from feeding upon the malignant pessimist or calamity mongers or weeping men, and prosperity for all our people will not be restored by the voluble wailings of word-sobbers nor by any legislative legerdemain proposed by theorists." He decided to abbreviate this note rather than give full throat to his fury.

Not until October 1930—a full year after the crash—did Hoover establish a President's Emergency Committee for Employment, and its main function was not to ease hardship but to create enough impression of motion to stave off growing demands for the dole. Modeled on the committee set up in the 1921 recession, it was headed by Colonel Arthur Woods, who had been in charge of the makeshift operation then. Though unemployment had climbed past the five million mark, the PECE did not give a penny to any local government for relief. Instead, it churned out press releases with pap topics such as urging people to hire men to "spruce up" their homes. Woods did not even try to collect trustworthy statistics on the extent of joblessness and of local resources. Asked by governors to send them the committee's plan to cope with unemployment, the PECE responded that it had no plan.

The flush of confidence in Hoover's program in the fall of 1929 had also dissipated. "We are living in a fool's paradise," the head of U.S. Steel told the American Iron and Steel Institute, "if we think every steel manufacturer in the United States has maintained . . . the current rates of wages." Frequently, when management did hold fast on wage rates, it reduced hours, so that weekly pay envelopes shrank. In 1930 factory payrolls plunged 35 percent; Detroit turned out two million fewer cars than it had the year before; and more than twenty-five thousand businesses failed—another unwelcome record. In these circumstances, Hoover's affirmations of success lost credibility. With unconscious humor, Simeon Fess, chairman of the Republican National Committee, stated in October 1930: "Persons high in Republican circles are beginning to believe that there is some concerted effort on foot to utilize the stock market as a method of discrediting the Administration. Every time an Administration official gives out an optimistic statement about business conditions, the market immediately drops."

• • •

In these dark hours, the nation looked to the president for guidance, comfort, and good cheer—but looked in vain. "If you want to get the gloomiest view of any subject on earth," his wife once said, "ask Bert about it." His blighted youth had taken a dreadful toll. Even in his final days, he still remembered "the harshness of Murdstone," and said of him and other Dickens characters, "I have met them alive many times in after years." Hoover, wrote a journalist who knew him well, "is charged with an essential unassuaged loneliness." Pessimism was his everyday companion. Gutzon Borglum, the sculptor of Mount Rushmore, said, "If you put a rose in Hoover's hand it would wilt."

Hoover saw no point in strutting on the stage to rally the nation. "You can't make a Teddy Roosevelt out of me," he told his staff. In his memoir *Forty-two Years in the White House*, the chief usher recalled that Hoover "would go about, never speaking to any of the help. Never a good-morning or even a nod of the head. Never a Merry Christmas or a Happy New Year. All days were alike to him. Sunday was no exception, for he worked just as hard on that day if not harder than on any of the others. There was always a frown on his face and a look of worry." He needed to devote himself wholly, Hoover believed, to scrutinizing economic events and devising remedies.

The president had no sense of how to reach out to a desperate nation. Hoover, observed Sir Wilmot Lewis, Washington correspondent of the *Times* of London, "can calculate wave lengths, but cannot see color. . . . He can understand vibrations but cannot hear tone." The biographer Henry Pringle thought Hoover "lamentably bad" when he spoke to large crowds because "inhibitions seem to rise in his throat and to choke his vocal cords." Pringle added: "He has not a single gesture. . . . He reads—his chin down against his shirt front—rapidly and quite without expression. . . . He can utter a striking phrase in so prosaic, so uninspired and so mumbling a fashion that it is completely lost on nine out of ten of his auditors." In his infrequent broadcasts, he droned on with no awareness of his unseen audience. As one analyst has observed, "To Hoover, the millions who listened over the radio were just eavesdroppers."

The country got its first opportunity to render a verdict on the president's policies in the November 1930 midterm elections, and the returns further disheartened Hoover. The administration could point out that the party in power usually loses seats in off-year contests, but that was whistling in the dark, for progressives had done well and Hoover loyalists had fared poorly. The Republicans' big majorities in Congress had been wiped out, with the GOP's seventeen-seat advantage in the U.S. Senate reduced to one. The party also lost fifty-two seats in the House, which, when the Seventy-second Congress convened in December 1931, Democrats would control for the first time since 1919. There was one other worrisome feature. In 1928 Franklin D. Roosevelt had barely slipped into the governorship of New York State with a 250,000 vote plurality. In 1930 he won reelection by three-quarters of a million votes, immediately becoming the front-runner to oppose Hoover in the next presidential race.

Instead of serving as an alarm siren, the election results hardened Hoover's determination to dig in his heels. When Woods strongly recommended that he ask Congress to appropriate several hundred million dollars for public works, Hoover ignored him. "The volume of construction work in the Government is already at the maximum limit warranted by financial prudence," he asserted in his December 1930 State of the Union message. "Prosperity," he declared, "cannot be restored by raids upon the public Treasury." He further incensed congressional Democrats by charging that they were "playing politics at the expense of human misery." Senator Robert F. Wagner of New York inquired what had happened to the man who had once favored public works planning for hard times.

Hoover also rejected Woods's advice to inform Congress that "our fellow citizens are facing a desperate emergency," with "our industrial system . . . in a grave, tragic, stupid and anomalous situation." Expressing pride that "local communities through their voluntary agencies have assumed the duty of relieving individual distress and are being generously supported by the public," Hoover said that there was "minimum actual suffering."

. . .

The State of the Union address came at a perilous moment when the financial system had begun to hemorrhage. In the last two months of 1930, six hundred banks failed. The shutdown of the Bank of United States on December 11 wiped out the life savings of four hundred thousand depositors, primarily Jewish garment workers—many of them recent immigrants who had placed their trust in an institution whose name suggested that it was an arm of the government. It was the worst collapse in the history of the republic.

These misfortunes reinforced the president's resolve to quiet anxieties in the financial community by balancing the budget. "The primary duty of the Government," said Hoover, who for so long had favored stimulating the economy, was "to hold expenditures within our income." Americans, he maintained, were "suffering . . . more from frozen confidence than . . . from frozen securities." To encourage investors, he sought to rein in the "big government" spenders. When Congress early in 1931 passed Senator Wagner's bill to rehabilitate the virtually useless United States Employment Service, his advisers (including Colonel Woods) urged Hoover to sign it, but he killed it with a pocket veto on the specious grounds that he wanted to "prevent a serious blow to labor during this crisis." Even the Republican press was appalled. One economist said, "It is not likely that any veto message of an American president ever exceeded this one in misstatements of fact," and another dismissed Hoover's rationalization as "one of the most dishonest documents I have ever read."

The year 1931 also saw rising anger at the president's attitude toward relief. Hoover continued to insist that communities were caring admirably for the impoverished at a time when over a million Americans were seeking refuge in freight cars—named derisively "Hoover Pullmans"—and when regiments living from hand to mouth were building shelters of scrap in empty lots in big cities—miserable shantytowns named "Hoovervilles." That winter the novelist Thomas Wolfe reported from New York: "I saw half naked wretches sitting on park benches at three in the morning in a freezing rain and sleet: often I saw a man and a woman huddled together with their arms around each other for warmth, and with sodden newspapers, rags, or anything they could find over their shoulders." A committee named by Hoover found "desperate distress" in Kentucky and West Virginia, with "deserving men, women, and children . . . suffering from hunger, exposure, and cold," and a Kentucky coal miner wrote: "We have been eating wild green. . . . Such as Polk salad, Violet tops, wild onions, forget me not wild lettuce and such weeds as cows eat as a cow wont eat a poison weeds." In April, recognizing that Hoover was doing next to nothing for the destitute, Woods quietly resigned.

As the PECE limped along without Woods, unemployment rose to eight million. In Chicago, behind high-priced restaurants, desperate men fought over leavings in garbage pails, and hundreds of women slept each night in Grant and Lincoln parks. Starting in April, Chicago's schoolteachers went without pay for eight of the following thirteen months. Though Hoover never wearied of citing the triumph of local initiative, the executive director of the Federation of Jewish Charities in Philadelphia reported to the annual convention of the National Conference of Social Work in June: "Private philanthropy is no longer capable of coping. . . . It is virtually bankrupt in the face of great disaster. With the bravest of intentions, the community chests . . . are altogether unequal to the task ahead of us."

By the middle of 1931, the man hailed on inauguration day as the "Great Engineer" had become the "Great Scrooge." In June, William Allen White wrote a novelist, "You bet I'll read your book. I see by the blurb that your heroine goes out west and falls in love with a mining engineer. She took an awful chance. America did that not long ago and now look at her." A month later, the White House correspondent of the *New York Times*, Arthur Krock, concluded: "Mr. Hoover thus far has failed as a party leader. He has failed as an economist. . . . He has failed as a business leader. . . . He has failed as a personality because of awkwardness of manner and speech and lack of mass magnetism."

During this spring, Hoover's agricultural program—the showpiece of his 1929 initiatives—ended in fiasco. Over the previous year the Grain Stabilization Corporation had been buying wheat, only to find that prices continued to tumble and that it was stuck with a huge store it could not readily dispose of. Purchasing cotton had a similar outcome; prices skidded from 17½¢ to 8¢—with no way to deal with a huge glut because Hoover refused to sanction production controls. The board eventually reached the point of urging growers to plow under every third row of cotton, but, as the historian Albert Romasco later wrote, "Despite the Farm Board's exertions to . . . sow among farmers the seeds of the new individualism, it succeeded in reaping only thistles and thorns."

In June the board gave up. Its Grain Stabilization Corporation stopped buying surpluses and dumped 257 million bushels on the market, driving down the price of wheat still further. From its $500 million revolving fund, the board had suffered losses of $345 million with nothing to show for it. Cotton prices eventually slumped to a sickening 4½¢ per pound. The government had financed the removal of 3.5 million bales from the market but saw 10 million bales added to the surfeit. After the board's capitulation, Hoover, who thought the government had already departed too far from sound principles, did nothing at all to sustain rural America. The farmer faced ruin and, because of his importance to the economy of Main Street, threatened to pull hundreds of banks down with him. Before Hoover's term was over, one-fourth of American farmers lost their holdings—their fields, their stock, their barns, their homes—some of which had been in one family for generations.

After the short session of Congress ended, Hoover turned aside pleas to bring legislators back, even though the Depression was worsening. "I do not propose to call an extra session of Congress," he announced in May. "I know of nothing that would so disturb the healing process now undoubtedly going on. . . . We cannot legislate ourselves out of a world economic depression." To believe that congressional action could speed recovery, Hoover told an Indianapolis gathering in June, resembled thinking that one could "exorcise a Caribbean hurricane by statutory law." So with Congress away from March 4 to December 7, 1931, Hoover assumed full responsibility for coping with hard times—and for all that went wrong.

Either out of conviction or in self-defense, Hoover increasingly offered a new explanation for why recovery was so slow in coming. "The major forces of the depression now lie outside of the United States," he had announced in December 1930, "and our recuperation has been retarded by the unwarranted degree of fear and apprehension created by these outside forces." In June 1931 he located the sources of these woes in "the malign inheritances in Europe of the Great War—its huge taxes, its mounting armament, its political and social instability, its disruption of economic life by the new boundaries." He had become so convinced of the validity of this hypothesis that he stated flatly, "Without the war we should have no . . . depression."

This reasoning had important implications. Two of them were advantageous to the president. Blaming Europe for the Depression liberated Hoover, never one to admit error, from acknowledging that the policies he was pursuing at home were languishing. In addition, he got high marks as a statesman for attempting to resolve problems abroad—especially on the Continent, which was encountering an acute financial panic in the spring of 1931. He was to find, however, that involving himself in overseas imbroglios only compounded his troubles.

8

Global Disorder

Herbert Hoover was the last American president to take office with no conspicuous need to pay attention to the rest of the world. Europe was convalescing. Asia was dormant. "It seems to me," he told his secretary of state, Henry Stimson, as they began to work together, "that there is the most profound outlook for peace today that we have had at any time in the last half century." But Hoover was not a lucky president. While grappling with the Great Depression, he had the misfortune of encountering a second crisis on his watch: the breakdown of the world order created at Versailles.

Aghast at the prospect of a return to the carnage in the trenches, statesmen in the period after the Great War had negotiated a number of accords. British prime minister Stanley Baldwin asked, "Who in Europe does not know that one more war in the West and the civilization of the ages will fall with as great a shock as that of Rome?" The Nine-Power Treaty of 1922 pledged signatories—among them Japan—to respect the territorial integrity of China, and committed them, if an alleged violation arose, to engage in "full and frank" discussion. Considerably more encompassing, at least in its pretension, was the Kellogg-Briand Pact of 1928. In putting their names to this multilateral treaty, the nations of the world—almost all of them—pledged to renounce war "as an instrument of national policy" and to settle "all . . . conflicts of whatever nature" amicably. Just two problems: the Nine-Power Treaty and accompanying naval agreements had no provision for inspection, the Kellogg-Briand Pact no mechanism for enforcement.

These deficiencies did not trouble Hoover in the least, for he was convinced that moral suasion would deter aggressors and that it was "contrary to the . . . best judgment of the United States to build peace on military sanctions." Indeed, he believed that the New World had a calling to teach that lesson to the Old. On Armistice Day, November 11, 1929, Hoover declared that "the European nations have, by the covenant of the League of Nations, agreed that if nations failed to settle their differences peaceably then force should be applied. . . . We have refused to travel this road. We are confident that at least in the Western hemisphere public opinion will suffice to check violence. This is the road we prepare to travel." Hoover had no perception of how fragile was the fabric of this "parchment peace."

Earlier in 1929, a squabble between China and the Soviet Union had exposed the Alice-in-Wonderland universe in which the Hoover administration conducted diplomacy. Stimson feared that the dispute would result in war, but he could not ask the League of Nations to resolve it because the United States was not a member. (Nor was the USSR.) The Nine-Power Treaty was inapplicable since Russia had not been a party to that agreement. So Stimson turned to the weak reed of the Kellogg-Briand Pact as a medium for admonishing the two powers, only to realize that he could not send a note to Moscow because the United States refused to recognize the Soviet regime.

Hoover sought to introduce rationality into international affairs by curbing expensive arms races—with the initial steps taken at a conference of five great powers in London in 1930. After three months of discussion, the parties agreed to scuttle some battleships and halt construction of capital ships for five years; safeguard merchant vessels from undersea attacks; and cap the tonnage of cruisers, destroyers, and submarines—the first time auxiliary vessels had ever been restricted. The historian Arnold Toynbee categorized the treaty as the "great outstanding international success of the year 1930."

In fact, the London conference fell far short of "success." When neither Hoover nor the British would agree to a consultative pact if France were attacked, the French bolted, as did the Italians—so the treaty was only a three-power document. Its main consequence was to strengthen chauvinism in Japan. Though the Japanese delegates extracted concessions on lesser vessels, they reaffirmed a 5–5–3 ratio for Britain, America, and Japan on capital ships. Hence, in signing the pact, they were acknowledging that in the most critical area their country was not the equal of the two great Western powers. When Admiral Takeshi Takarabe returned to Japan, a political science student went to his home, read a protest against the treaty, then drew out a hidden dagger and committed hara-kiri. That fall a young fanatic shot Prime Minister Osachi Hamaguchi.

Despite the shortcomings of the London meetings, Hoover had nearly visionary expectations of the World Disarmament Conference that convened in Geneva early in 1932. (*Disarmament* was an extravagant term for arms reduction.) He urged a one-third cutback in "armies in excess of the level required to preserve internal order," as well as "abolition of certain 'aggressive' arms"; advocated cuts of 25 percent in aircraft carriers, cruisers, and destroyers, and of 33 percent in battleships and submarines; and demanded the elimination of tanks, poison gas, bombers, and heavy mobile artillery. Hoover thought that outlawing tanks would help national economies by cutting needless expenses. In scolding France for devoting a large proportion of its budget to arms, Hoover was looking only at cost sheets with no sensitivity to why the French, having twice within memory been invaded from the east, might think it prudent to erect defenses against the prospect of a resurgent Germany—particularly since Nazis had made alarming gains in recent elections. When Hoover left office, the delegates had gotten nowhere. The Geneva conference, wrote the diplomatic historian Robert Ferrell later, was "an unmitigated nuisance."

. . .

The president felt more in his element in the Western Hemisphere. On November 19, 1928, only two weeks after the election, he set off on a voyage of friendship to ten Latin American nations. From Amapala, Honduras, to Montevideo, Uruguay, he repeatedly expressed his desire to be a "good neighbor"—more than four years before FDR used that phrase. In Nicaragua, Hoover told the leaders of two hostile factions that he planned to end Uncle Sam's military presence in their country. Holding true to that pledge, he refused to send forces into the interior—even when incursions by the anti-American rebel August Sandino, who Hoover thought "a bandit beyond the pale," took American lives. On January 2, 1933, the last detachment of marines pulled out of Nicaragua.

Hoover's policies implied a revised conception of the Monroe Doctrine. This reconsideration had been foreshadowed shortly before he took office in a memorandum prepared by Undersecretary of State J. Reuben Clark repudiating the Roosevelt Corollary of 1904, which justified intervention in Latin American republics guilty of "chronic wrongdoing." The Monroe Doctrine, Stimson declared, was a "declaration of the U.S. versus Europe—not of the U.S. versus Latin America." Rejecting Wilson's requirement that governments must meet certain moral standards in order to be granted recognition, Hoover dealt with any de facto regime that established its authority.

The more than twenty insurrections that erupted in Latin America during Hoover's four years strongly tested his resolve. So, too, did regimes that repeatedly angered U.S. investors by defaulting on bonds. But Hoover, for the most part, exercised restraint. His administration recognized an insurgent junta in Bolivia despite its anti-American tendencies, and when the U.S. minister to Costa Rica, in the midst of an uprising, asked for two warships, he was turned down. Hoover did not even blink an eye when a revolution flared up in Panama near the indispensable canal. *Mundo al Día* of Bogotá rejoiced that the Monroe Doctrine, "a historical relic," had become no more than an "irritating anachronism," and *La Prensa* in Buenos Aires commented, "Mr. Hoover differs from other American Presidents in not proclaiming any God-given mission over the rest of the continent."

Neither Hoover nor the State Department wholly abandoned paternalism, however. Historians have made more of the Clark memorandum, which got little notice during his presidency, than Hoover did. On three occasions the Hoover administration used the threat of intervention to compel Dominican leaders to behave, and Stimson, at one point, referred to Bolivia and Paraguay as "those two little nonsensical republics." Early in his presidency, Hoover resolved to end U.S. control of Haiti as well, but he could not quite pull it off. The State Department dragged its feet, and the Haitian national assembly unanimously rejected a treaty that retained some American financial authority. Hoover did replace the U.S. military commissioner with a civilian and in other actions speeded withdrawal. But when he left office, American troops still garrisoned Haiti. As a consequence, Franklin Roosevelt got the credit for terminating the occupation, though Hoover had gone a long way toward making that possible.

By recognizing despots who repressed dissent, Hoover eliminated any need for intervention in civil strife and fostered a business climate congenial to American investors. In El Salvador, following an army coup that provoked what Stimson termed "a rather nasty proletarian revolution," Hoover sent three warships to support the government, which enjoyed his backing even after it massacred thirty thousand peasants. In Nicaragua, Stimson endorsed the strongman Anastasio Somoza, who was friendly toward U.S. corporations in the banana republic. (In 1934, during FDR's presidency, Somoza arranged for the cold-blooded murder of Sandino, and as late as 1979 the Somoza family was still running Nicaragua as a fiefdom—with U.S. acquiescence.) Ironically, Nicaragua had free elections just once—when marines, agents of the overbearing *yanquis*, monitored polling places. Liberals, who had been vocal opponents of imperialism, wound up finding fault with Hoover not for meddling, but for failing to take advantage of American might to dislodge brutal dictators.

The president met with only partial success south of the border. The Hawley-Smoot tariff engendered bitter resentment, and intellectuals raged against the financial towers of Manhattan. Latin America would be better off, said a Mexican philosopher, "if the blast of a cataclysm should sweep away the skyscrapers and the Island were to return to the ploughing of its smiling meadows in the period of the Dutch engravings." Yet Hoover's policies did mark a departure. If he was not the creator of the Good Neighbor Policy, he was, at least, its godfather.

• • •

Hoover found Asia much more difficult terrain. Though the United States was committed to preserving the territorial integrity of China, he shared the sentiments of a friend who wrote him, "I think the Japs are our first line of the defense in the Far East; and I am certainly glad they are well armed." Hoover looked much less favorably on China, for which he had developed contempt in his mining days, than on Japan—an advanced industrial country that could impose order on the fractious Orient. It was not unreasonable, he told his cabinet, for the Japanese to believe that they needed to safeguard their land from "a Bolshevist Russia to the north and a possible Bolshevist China" to the west.

A clash between Japanese and Chinese soldiers north of Mukden in Manchuria on the night of September 18, 1931, has come to be perceived as the opening shot of World War II—much like Sarajevo in 1914—but initially neither Hoover nor anyone else saw reason for concern. Details were murky, and the conflict over the South Manchurian Railway Line did not measure up to a clear-cut invasion of China by Japan: the Chinese had not established sovereignty over the region, and the Japanese owned the railroad. Furthermore, since Japan regarded this area as within its sphere of influence—much as Western powers laid claim to the Caribbean—the United States could view the episode from the perspective of realpolitik. "President Hoover and his Cabinet were becoming more and more absorbed in the domestic economic situation," an American diplomat later recalled. "They felt very sincerely that it was no time for the Chinese to be shrieking bloody murder under their windows."

Not until Japan moved toward devouring all of Manchuria did Hoover recognize that "the Mukden incident" had evolved into "the Far Eastern Crisis," and even then he moved circumspectly. With militarists poised to take over the government in Tokyo, Stimson concluded that "the situation is in the hands of virtually mad dogs," but Hoover counseled forbearing. His years in Asia had taught him that China swallows its invaders—or disgorges them. Instead of threatening economic sanctions, he favored assuring Tokyo that they would not be imposed, because he did not want to do anything that might bolster Japanese jingos. Boycott, he believed, was "the surest way into war."

The Manchurian quagmire offered by far the greatest challenge that had ever been posed to the Versailles system, but the Western powers showed no disposition to take it on. Suspecting that the League of Nations—and more particularly Britain and France—wanted to burden the United States with the responsibility of confronting Japan, both Hoover and Stimson were determined not to permit "anybody to deposit that baby on our lap." The president did authorize the American consul at Geneva, Prentiss Gilbert, to be an observer when the League Council discussed Manchuria, but Gilbert's participation was as rigidly prescribed as that of a thespian in a tableau. After first instructing Gilbert to hunker along the wall, Stimson relented and let him sit at "the damned table," but he was still ordered to "keep his mouth shut."

Unwilling to approve either military or economic sanctions, Hoover still sought some way to compel Tokyo to relent. In November 1931 he proposed to Stimson an announcement that the United States would not recognize any territorial acquisition resulting from aggression—an idea borrowed from former secretary of state William Jennings Bryan, who had first employed the tactic in response to a Japanese ultimatum to China in 1915. Subjected to "the searchlight of public opinion" and to "moral influence," Japan, Hoover explained, would be told that if she did not desist, "she'll be an outlaw nation."

In January 1932 Stimson, with Hoover's approval, sent identical notes to Japan and China announcing that the American government did not "intend to recognize any . . . agreement . . . which may impair the treaty rights of the United States or its citizens in China, including those which relate to the . . . territorial . . . integrity of the Republic of China, or to . . . the open door policy." Nor did it "intend to recognize any . . . agreement . . . brought about by means contrary to the covenants" of the Kellogg-Briand Pact. Thus was born what came to be known as the "Stimson Doctrine."

Stimson underscored this message with public letters in February and September to the chairman of the Senate Foreign Relations Committee, William Borah, and in August with an address to the Council on Foreign Relations. In his first communication to Borah, he stated that if Japan persisted in violating the Washington treaties of 1922, including the Nine-Power Pact, the United States would no longer be bound by any commitments it had made in these agreements and would feel free to fortify bases in the western Pacific and to enlarge its navy.

The Stimson Doctrine has had a curious afterlife. Hoover subsequently wrote that Stimson was more a "warrior than a diplomat," and Stimson asserted that Hoover had been enfeebled by his Quaker upbringing. But both men—and the historians who followed these leads—were exaggerating their differences. The secretary of state was more willing than the president to try to bluff the Japanese by threats and to give some consideration to sanctions, but neither favored unilateral steps that might lead to war. Partisans also differed over authorship of the nonrecognition notes, which Hoover claimed "would take rank with the greatest papers of this country." His champions contended that, given the president's role in their origin, the appropriate nomenclature was "the

Hoover-Stimson Doctrine." Ironically, they were bickering over which man deserved "credit" for a procedure that was a manifest failure. The Japanese treated Stimson's protest with contempt.

The bankruptcy of policy in Asia provides an important explanation for why a 2007 poll of more than one thousand international relations faculty across the United States and Canada ranked Hoover as the worst president of the twentieth century on foreign affairs. By failing to draw the line in Manchuria, historians have said, he gave aggressors in Berlin, Rome, and Tokyo a green light. He had floated into office on a sea of tranquillity and departed with Adolf Hitler in power, the Reichstag in ashes, and the Japanese careening unhindered down the road that would dead-end at Pearl Harbor. Hoover has even been accused of paving the way to World War II.

This arraignment is tendentious, even overwrought. True, Hoover did not do well abroad. On one occasion, Stimson noted in his diary, "The President is so absorbed with the domestic situation that he told me frankly that he can't think very much now of foreign affairs." Hoover's concentration on economic considerations—almost to the total exclusion of political and strategic concerns—was myopic, and his reliance on public opinion as a deterrent was naive. Yet no president during the interwar years—no matter how internationalist his perspective—could diverge very far from the ingrained and all but immobilizing isolationism of the American people, as Franklin Roosevelt was to discover. (More generous than some scholars, FDR thought "old Hoover's foreign policy has been pretty good.") Disillusioned by participation in the Great War, battered by the Great Depression, the nation would never have supported a war on behalf of Manchuria.

Furthermore, narrow though his conception of foreign policy was, Hoover had good reason to be engrossed in economic predicaments—especially a financial meltdown in the heart of Europe. On May 11, 1931, Kreditanstalt, the greatest bank in Austria, buckled. The announcement from Vienna that the mainstay of the valley of the Danube had been drained of its resources sent shock waves through Mitteleuropa. German president Paul

von Hindenburg, fearful that cascading bank failures would pre-
cipitate a Communist or Fascist coup in his country, sent a personal plea to the American leader. "All possibilities of improving
the situation by domestic measures without relief from abroad
are exhausted," he wrote Hoover. With major U.S. banks having
invested close to half their capital in German securities, Wall
Street became frantic. "Apprehension," Hoover later said, "began
to run like mercury through the financial world." Hoover's own
mood, Stimson noted, was "pure indigo." After one White House
meeting, the secretary of state set down in his diary: "The President . . . went through all the blackest surmises. . . . It was like
sitting in a bath of ink to sit in his room."

Hoover, however, rebounded with the boldest initiative of his
presidency. On June 20, 1931, at a time when J. P. Morgan was saying that the American government needed to toss "a life-saver for
the world," Hoover recommended a one-year moratorium on payment of the war debts European powers owed the United States,
with the understanding that during this period they, in turn, would
suspend collection of the annual reparations from Germany imposed at Versailles. He embarked on this course despite strenuous
opposition from Secretary of the Treasury Mellon and warnings
that he was encroaching on the constitutional prerogatives of Congress. "This is perhaps the most daring statement I ever thought of
issuing," he confided to his press secretary. To supplement his action on intergovernmental debts, Hoover also dragooned bankers
into accepting a "standstill" agreement that they would not, for a
time, demand payment on private loans to Germans.

Though Hoover's endeavor earned him plaudits in unlikely quarters, it failed to stanch the crumpling of the international financial
system. The Nation, often unfriendly to Hoover, called his intervention "probably . . . the most far-reaching and . . . praiseworthy step
taken by an American President since the treaty of peace." With a
vigor Washington had not seen from him before, Hoover pressed
members of both parties to support the moratorium. "For the first
time since he has been president," Senator Norris said, "he has com-

municated with me." But in July the second biggest bank in Germany folded, and in September, to Hoover's consternation, Great Britain abandoned the gold standard.

London's momentous decision had serious repercussions across the Atlantic. At a time when America badly needed anti-deflationary measures, the Fed abruptly tightened credit in order to halt the flow of gold out of the country, and the president's determination to slash government spending drastically became an obsession. Hoover had hoped that the moratorium would win a year "to help free the recuperative forces already in motion in the United States from retarding influences abroad." The main impact of the Kreditanstalt crisis, however, was not that it led to Hoover's commendable engagement abroad, but that it rigidified government policies, worsening the Great Depression at home.

9

Defeat

In October 1931, Hoover returned to Philadelphia for another World Series contest at Shibe Park—where two years earlier he had received such a heartwarming welcome—only to be greeted by deafening boos. The City of Brotherly Love had turned nasty for more than one reason. As raucous chants of "We want beer!" indicated, the president was out of step with the rising resentment toward Prohibition. More important, a Philadelphia authority soon reported, "We have unemployment in every third house. It is almost like the visitation of death to the households of the Egyptians at the time of the escape of the Jews from Egypt." And on the very day of the game, one of the city's largest banks, the Franklin Trust Company, collapsed—the consequence, a state official said, of "the hysteria and unfavorable psychological reaction which are gripping the public."

The affliction that brought down Franklin Trust felled scores of other financial institutions. Within a month after Britain jettisoned the gold standard, 522 U.S. banks failed, and that autumn, in the greatest outflow of bullion in American history, $1 billion were removed from bank vaults and squirreled away in coffeepots, mattresses, and other hiding places. No longer was anyone saying "as safe as a bank."

The night before Hoover went to Shibe Park to watch Connie Mack's A's take on the Cards, he had made his way to Andrew Mellon's palatial mansion on Massachusetts Avenue for a secret session with the country's foremost financiers. The president beseeched the bankers to create a credit pool to assist weaker institutions and was shocked when, instead of manifesting determination to preserve private authority, they asked for government intervention. Only after he promised federal action if voluntary efforts failed would they agree to set up a National Credit Corporation with a fund of $500 million.

The National Credit Corporation did next to nothing. Focused understandably on maintaining the liquidity of their own institutions, the House of Morgan and other mammoths considered it imprudent to throw good money after bad. They demanded collateral that only a bank with little or no need for assistance could provide. By December the NCC had parted with a paltry $10 million. When 1931 came to an end, a reckoning found that over the course of the year nearly 2,300 banks had closed their doors, a historic milestone— almost twice as many as in 1930. Hoover concluded from the misadventure not that his faith in voluntarism required rethinking, but that bankers were a shabby lot.

While the NCC was self-destructing, Hoover's program launched in the fall of 1929 to rely on big business to sustain labor was further disintegrating. U.S. Steel announced it was cutting wage rates 10 percent, and major firms such as General Motors and U.S. Rubber quickly followed its lead. Henry Ford, acclaimed as the apostle of high wages, slashed rates, and the Ford Motor Company had already fired three out of every four workers. At a time when Hoover was trumpeting the superiority of free enterprise over foreign systems, the Soviet Union publicized six thousand job openings; a hundred thousand Americans applied.

In August 1931, Hoover had replaced the defunct Woods outfit with a President's Organization on Unemployment Relief chaired by the head of American Telephone and Telegraph, Walter S. Gifford.

Though POUR had a different name and acronym than PECE, it was essentially the same organization and just as feckless. According to Will Rogers's facetious account, Hoover approached Gifford by telling him he had a remarkable task for him to take on. "Why is it remarkable?" Gifford inquired. "Because we are giving you no resources to do it with," the president replied. The creation of another committee—a shopworn Hoover palliative—was intended, he made clear, to silence the cries for "a socialistic dole."

Hoover took POUR no more seriously than its predecessor. Gifford had hardly accepted the assignment, which he did not want, when the president again pontificated that reports of unemployment were exaggerated. Demoralized, several members of POUR's staff resigned. A still lower point for the operation came when Gifford was compelled to admit at a Senate committee hearing that he had no idea how many people needed relief or how many were getting it. He did not believe, he told his interrogators, that "the data would be of any particular value." He added, "My sober and considered judgment is that . . . Federal aid would be a disservice to the unemployed."

• • •

Gifford's statements dovetailed with those of the president. In his State of the Union address in December 1931, Hoover insisted, "Our people are providing against distress from unemployment in true American fashion by magnificent response to public appeal and by action of the local governments." He opposed "any . . . dole" because, thanks to "the sense of social responsibility in the Nation, our people have been protected from hunger and cold," and voluntary effort gave "assurance against suffering during the coming winter." When Hoover wrote these words, more than two hundred thousand men and women were walking the streets of Detroit seeking work. Throughout the country, tar-paper Hoovervilles were multiplying; one ragtag community of the dispossessed squatted in Manhattan's Central Park. Although Hoover claimed "nobody actually starved," the commissioner of charity in Salt Lake City reported that, after county and private relief funds gave out, families were slowly starving. The historian Irving Bernstein later noted the death from starvation of a four-year-old boy in Oakland, California, and of a man in a barn near Troy, New York. In 1931 New York City hospitals recorded scores of such deaths: Gouverneur, one; Harlem, two; Kings County, thirty-three; Bellevue, fifty-nine. Outside the White House, Communist demonstrators sang, "We'll hang Herbie Hoover to a sour apple tree."

Alarmed that the government was running a historic deficit—nearly a billion dollars—Hoover believed it essential to balance the budget in order to forestall a run on gold reserves and to instill faith in the integrity of the government. "Nothing will contribute more to the return of prosperity than to maintain the sound fiscal position of the Federal Government," he declared in the address. Consequently, he advocated substantial tax increases along with cuts in government spending—precisely the wrong medicine for the ailing economy.

Yet in this same message preaching austerity and minimalist government, Hoover asked Congress for speedy action to resuscitate the War Finance Corporation, though doing so involved unprecedented federal intervention in peacetime and vast expenditures. New York's fiery representative Fiorello La Guardia denounced the legislation as "a millionaire's dole," and Senator Norris said, "I have been called a socialist, a Bolshevik, a communist, and a lot of other terms of similar nature, but in the wildest flights of my imagination I never thought of such a thing as putting the Government into business as far as this bill would put it in." So frightening, though, were bulletins on the imperiled financial system that in January 1932 Congress chartered the Reconstruction Finance Corporation (the wartime agency under a new name) to lend money to banks, railroads, insurance firms, building and loan associations, and other institutions. Started with $500 million in capital, the RFC was authorized to make available, through issue of securities, four times that sum for a total of $2 billion—a staggering amount. Bankers, remarked Will Rogers, had "the honor of being the first group to go on the 'dole' in America."

Progressives found it impossible to square Hoover's RFC venture with his adamant refusal to sanction federal relief or with his earlier record abroad as a humanitarian. "We shall help the railroad; we shall help the financial institutions; and I agree that we should," Senator Robert Wagner stated. "But is there any reason why we should not likewise extend a helping hand to that forlorn American, in every village and every city of the United States, who has been without wages since 1929? Must he alone carry the cross of individual responsibility?" Remarking on the eagerness of the government to bail out bankers, he added: "We did not preach to them rugged individualism. We did not sanctimoniously roll out sentences rich with synonyms of self-reliance. We were not carried away with apprehension over what would happen to their independence if we extended them a helping hand." The columnist Heywood Broun underscored another anomaly. "The only mistake starving unemployed of this country have made," he wrote, "is that they did not march on Washington and under the windows of Mr. Hoover in the White House display . . . banners reading 'We are Belgians.'"

Hoover accompanied his request for an RFC with a number of other initiatives. He asked Congress to augment the capital of Federal Land banks and to establish a system of Home Loan Discount banks that would undergird mortgages. More important was the Glass-Steagall bill to ease credit by liberalizing requirements for the issue of Federal Reserve notes. *Business Week* regarded it as "perhaps the most powerful dose of monetary medicine that has ever been applied to the strengthening of the banking system in a similar period of time," and Hoover promoted it as a "national defense measure" to save the gold standard. With Republicans and hardshell Democrats allied, the House took only ten minutes, the Senate a mere three, to approve the bill in late February. "This isn't a session of Congress," complained La Guardia. "This is a kissing bee!"

Commentators marveled at Hoover's change of heart toward

mobilizing the national government, but he had undergone no fundamental transformation. He made these recommendations only because he had lost faith in public-spirited bankers and had run out of other options for thawing sources of credit. Gratified that the agency was only temporary, Hoover took the RFC legislation as a bad-tasting pill. Historians who later portrayed Hoover as a proto–New Dealer misconceived his point of view. Only unwittingly—by revealing the inadequacy of his voluntaristic approach—was Hoover the progenitor of FDR's enlargement of federal authority.

The RFC got off to a good start, but the hope that it would bring about recovery soon withered. By lending hundreds of millions of dollars to financial institutions, it reduced bank closings from 346 in January to 46 in April; however, before the year was out, 140 banks that had received RFC loans shut their doors. The agency also failed to jump-start the economy. Instead of seizing upon the RFC as a way to stimulate business by expanding credit, many bankers saw an opportunity to shore up their holdings. Furthermore, manufacturers were not eager to go further into debt by producing goods for which there was a shrinking market.

Without any effective galvanizer, the slump dramatically worsened—erasing all the gains of the golden era of Hoover's public career. Factories in 1932 turned out less than they had in 1913. For every four cars that rolled off the assembly line in 1929, only one emerged in 1932. Steel plants operated at a pitiful 11 percent of capacity. And with few jobs to be had, breadlines grew longer. The business magazine *Fortune* estimated that 34 million men, women, and children were "without any income whatever," and this figure "omitted America's 11 million farm families, who were suffering in a rural Gethsemane of their own."

Hoover and his circle cocooned themselves from the magnitude of the deprivation. The president marshaled statements from the surgeon general claiming that the health of the nation was better in the Great Depression than it had been in prosperous years—proving, Hoover said, that "our people have been protected from hunger and cold." He circulated comforting hearsay: "The hoboes . . . are better fed than they have ever been. One hobo in New York got ten meals in one day." Social workers sat seething while Secretary of the Interior Wilbur told their national convention that "our children are apt to profit, rather than suffer, from what is going on," since in hard times parents were more attentive and the young got "better and more suitable food than in past good times." Private charity and local governments, Hoover continued to insist, were performing splendidly in seeing that no one was in want—a contention he maintained even when, in the spring of 1932, *Business Week* was writing of "complete breakdown."

Community chests could deal with a few hundred out of work, perhaps a few thousand, but they could not conceivably meet the needs of a city such as Cleveland, where 50 percent of the workforce was jobless. In Akron and East St. Louis, unemployment reached 60 percent; in Toledo it mounted to 80 percent. Even cities not so hard hit fell far short. In North Carolina's capital, the Raleigh Community Chest allowed a destitute family a nickel a day for food.

Investigators found that Hoover's reliance on municipalities was also ill founded. One hundred cities in 1932 appropriated no money at all for the indigent. New York City had twenty-five thousand emergency cases on its waiting list, and no way to help them. The city of Houston announced shamelessly: "Applications are not taken from unemployed Mexican or colored families. They are being asked to shift for themselves." Chicago separated families, sending husbands and wives to different shelters. When Detroit, where unemployment was nearing a quarter of a million, exhausted its funds, bankers told the city that, to qualify for loans, it must drop more than one-third of its families from the relief rolls. The vice chairman of the Mayor's Unemployment Commission of Detroit saw "no possibility of preventing widespread hunger and slow starvation." A Philadelphia storekeeper reported: "Eleven children in that house. They've got no shoes, no pants. In the house, no chairs. My God, you go in there, you cry, that's all."

Single-mindedly, Hoover concentrated not on aid to the bereft but on balancing the budget. Whatever members of Congress proposed—not only federal relief, but modest efforts such as gathering statistics on job loss or modernizing employment exchanges—he set himself sternly against. "We cannot . . . squander ourselves into prosperity," he admonished. On May 31, 1932, he took the unusual step of appearing in the U.S. Senate chamber to scold legislators for considering costly relief and public works measures. "The course of unbalanced budgets is the road to ruin," he declared. Instead, to pare the deficit, he urged Congress to raise taxes. That plea resulted in the Revenue Act of 1932—a law that, ever since, has been condemned by economists for draining purchasing power.

So great was the pressure from progressives in both parties for aid to the jobless, though, that Hoover capitulated and in July signed the Emergency Relief and Construction Act. The law provided $300 million in loans to states for succoring "needy and distressed people" and empowered the RFC to finance $1.5 billion for income-producing public works such as toll roads. In addition, it authorized over $300 million for emergencies. Never before had Congress enacted a statute of this nature or of these dimensions.

At Hoover's behest, however, RFC officials administered the law so stingily that the tens of thousands of jobs the country had been promised were never created. "These loans are to be based upon absolute need and evidence of financial exhaustion," the president said. "I do not expect any state to resort to it except as a last extremity." When the governor of Pennsylvania asked for enough money to give those who were down-and-out thirteen cents a day, the RFC granted a sum that permitted just three cents a day. By mid-October, the RFC had approved only three of the 243 applications it had received for public works projects. That was not the kind of record likely to be helpful to Hoover as he appealed to a beleaguered nation for another term in office.

· · ·

No episode in his presidency, though, so fixed in the mind of America the conviction that Hoover was cold and heartless as his treatment of "the bonus army." In the spring of 1932, veterans of the Great War congregated in Washington in hope of persuading Congress to approve immediate payment of bonuses for their service—funds they were scheduled to receive years later but desperately needed in grim times. After the Senate rejected their request in June, most of the demonstrators left town. Several thousand, though, remained—in a settlement outside of the city at Anacostia Flats and in unoccupied government buildings along Pennsylvania Avenue. On July 28, following a melee downtown, Hoover—insensitive to how his action might appear—ordered the U.S. Army to rout the squatters and to confine the rest of the bonus marchers in the Flats.

The drama moved on in unforeseen ways. Mounted cavalrymen—sabers drawn—led six tanks and a detachment of infantrymen with fixed bayonets down Pennsylvania Avenue to a site not far from the Capitol, where they met no resistance. In flagrant violation of the president's orders, the overbearing chief of staff, General Douglas MacArthur, then moved to drive the veterans and their families out of their squalid encampment in Anacostia Flats in the middle of the night. Cavalry harried the former doughboys; tanks rolled through their tent village; and infantry prodded them with bayonets, fired tear-gas canisters, and torched their shelters.

For days and weeks thereafter, newspapers and magazines raged against the president; movie audiences, shocked by newsreel footage of the mayhem, hissed when Hoover's face appeared on the screen. "I swear I could not believe it," wrote the popular syndicated columnist Floyd Gibbons. "The victims are American citizens, veteran soldiers, some of them disabled men who fought to sustain this Government." In like manner, the *Washington News* told its readers, "What a pitiful spectacle is that of the great American Government, mightiest in the world, chasing unarmed men, women and children with army tanks." Even more irate was the Hearst press. "For sheer stupidity," concluded the *San Francisco Examiner*, "President Hoover's spectacular employment of the military in evicting a mere handful of the derelicts of the World War from their wretched billets in Washington is without parallel in American annals."

Journalists offered vivid details, which, for decades, unwary historians have repeated. Hoover was portrayed as a murderer, though the army never fired a shot. The two veterans who died that day were killed not by soldiers but in self-defense by District police. The Pulitzer Prize–winning reporter Paul Y. Anderson gave an "eyewitness" account of an "eleven-weeks-old baby in a grave condition from gas, shock and exposure; one eight-year-old boy partly blinded by gas; . . . one bystander shot through the shoulder, one veteran's ear severed with a cavalry saber." Every allegation false. Hoover was blamed especially for the death in Anacostia of an infant, who, it was said, had succumbed to tear gas. The bonus marchers' *News* proposed an epitaph: "Here lies Bernard Myers, aged three months, gassed to death by order of President Hoover." In fact, the baby had died of pneumonia after his parents refused medical treatment. Nor was there a word of truth in the story that "a boy received a bayonet thrust in the thigh while rushing back to get his rabbit." Even MacArthur's vainglory was exaggerated—hard though that was to do. These atrocity tales, the historian Roger Daniels has observed, "fit quite well into the old Christian tradition of the massacre of the innocents with poor Herbert Hoover badly miscast as Herod."

The reality, however, was bad enough. Instead of rebuking MacArthur for his insubordination, Hoover joined him in claiming, despite all the evidence to the contrary, that there was an "extraordinary proportion of criminal, communist and non-veteran elements amongst the marchers." Moreover, though stories of army behavior were embroidered, cavalrymen did flail with both flat and point of their sabers, and infantrymen fired some 1,500 rounds of tear gas. The highly regarded journalist Thomas L. Stokes reflected on the burning of Anacostia: "My mood was one of despair. It was an experience that stands apart from all others in my life. So all the misery and suffering had finally come to this—soldiers marching with their guns against American citizens. I had nothing but bitter feelings toward Herbert Hoover that night." One American appalled by the violence was the man the Democratic Party had just chosen to oppose Hoover in November. "Well," Franklin Roosevelt told an adviser, "this elects me."

• • •

As the 1932 campaign got under way, few observers saw even a glimmer of possibility that the president would win a second term. The election, stated a Richmond editor, was going to be "an inquest" at which "the American people will sit as a coroner's jury, and . . . bring in their verdict against Herbert Hoover." The Republican convention hall in Chicago displayed no picture of the president. "If the election was held tomorrow," a former Oregon governor said, "any Democratic candidate who had not been convicted of anything more than rape or murder would defeat Mr. Hoover."

Unhappily for Hoover, the Democrats had picked a formidable nominee, though it took some time for the president to acknowledge that. Hoover initially rejoiced in the Democrats' choice, for he thought Franklin D. Roosevelt was the weakest candidate in the field. When FDR lost the Massachusetts primary, Hoover was downcast because he feared it meant that Roosevelt would not be his opponent. Even when Hoover did recognize that the ebullient governor of the country's most populous state was no pushover, he failed to comprehend that his rival's attitude toward help for the impoverished would give FDR the advantage. Roosevelt had told the New York legislature that relief "must be extended by Government, not as a matter of charity, but as a matter of social duty; the State accepts the task cheerfully because it believes that it will help restore that close relationship with its people which is necessary to preserve our democratic form of government."

In contrast, Hoover ran as a right-winger of deepest dye. Not a trace of his earlier progressivism could be discerned. In his final months in office, he sealed the impression of himself as a dogmatic reactionary. Some of his comments were hysterical. At a time when liberals were disappointed by Roosevelt's moderation, Hoover charged that FDR's approach incarnated "the same philosophy of government which has poisoned all Europe . . . the fumes of the witch's cauldron which boiled in Russia."

Hoover conducted a lackluster campaign. No one applauded at the end of his acceptance address, because, reported a British journalist, of "the dispiriting influence of Mr. Hoover's personality, his unprepossessing exterior, his sour, puckered face of a bilious baby, his dreary, nasal monotone reading interminably, and, for the most part inaudibly, from a typescript without a single inflection of a voice or gesture to relieve the tedium." Only once did he leaven his stupefying recitals of statistics with a ray of wit—in Cleveland when, remarking on how frequently his opponent shifted positions, he likened Roosevelt to a "chameleon on . . . plaid."

The president had planned to give only three addresses, but when on September 12, 1932, reliably Republican Maine, which voted early in local races, lurched Democratic, he realized that FDR could no longer be taken lightly. "It is a catastrophe for us," he said. "The thing for us to do is to carry the fight right to Roosevelt. . . . We have got to crack him every time he opens his mouth." Later that month, bewailing the "hatred" for him that pervaded the West, he declared that "the only possibility of winning the election, which is lost now, would be exciting a fear of what Roosevelt would do."

No longer did the nation hail Hoover as the Great Engineer. "No other man could, possibly, have done more; but no other man could conceivably have done less," stated a New Haven paper. "The country is pretty tired of the Hoover myth." The *New Republic* editor Robert Morss Lovett wrote: "Never before in this country has government fallen to so low a place in popular estimation, or been so universally an object of cynical contempt. Never before has the chief magistrate given his name so liberally to latrines and offal dumps, or had his face banished from the screen to avoid the hoots and jeers of children." War veterans circulated a parody:

> Hoover is our shepherd
> We are in want
> He maketh us to lie
> Down on the park benches
> He leadeth us beside the still factories
> He disturbeth our soul.

Stories circulated that he had accumulated a fortune from the distress of the Belgians, that dogs took an instinctive dislike to him, even that he had conspired in kidnapping and murdering the Lindbergh baby. Drawing upon the conviction that Hoover was an agent of the Crown, signs urged the destitute to "Eat 'erbs with 'Erbie," and a radical farm leader denounced him as "the foreigner in the White House." One vicious diatribe, John Hamill's *The Strange Career of Mr. Hoover Under Two Flags*, reached number six on Macy's list of nonfiction best sellers, though it was a tissue of lies.

When the Republican campaign train rolled into Detroit, where many thousands of autoworkers had been discharged, angry crowds shook their fists at the president and chanted, "Hang Hoover! Hang Hoover! Hang Hoover!" Placards read "Down with Hoover, Slayer of Veterans." To protect him from the furor, mounted police had to be summoned. "I've been travelling with presidents since Theodore Roosevelt's time, and never before have I seen one actually booed, with men running out into the streets to thumb their noses at him," a Secret Service agent said. "It's not a pretty sight."

His face ashen, his eyes bloodshot, his hands trembling, Hoover soldiered on, convinced that he carried the fate of the republic with him. But when, on the final day of October, he approached Madison Square Garden, cries of "We want bread!" rang in his ears. "This campaign is more than a contest between two men," he declared in his opening sentence. "It is a contest between two philosophies." Paraphrasing, curiously, William Jennings Bryan, he warned that if the country jettisoned the protective tariff, "the grass will grow in the streets of a hundred cities, a thousand towns; the weeds will overrun the fields of millions of farms. . . . Their churches, their hospitals, and schoolhouses will decay." He concluded: "This election is not a mere shift from the ins to the outs. It means deciding the direction our Nation will take over a century to come."

As the campaign ground toward a close, Hoover—his prematurely white hair unkempt, his clothes disheveled, his voice all but gone—found it increasingly hard to go through the motions. His press secretary later wrote of his appearance in St. Paul: "He spoke haltingly and without emphasis. . . . He lost his place in the manuscript again and again. . . . A man sat directly behind him gripping an empty chair throughout the time he was speaking, so that, if he should collapse, the chair could be pushed under him and he would not fall to the platform." Hoover also misjudged the temper of the country, even at a friendly party rally in Minnesota. In what was taken to be an allusion to his handling of the bonus marchers, he ad-libbed, "Thank God, we still have some officials in Washington that can hold out against a mob." The audience gasped.

His final campaign leg—west to California—painfully exposed the country's animus toward him. In Wisconsin his train was halted after a man was detected extracting spikes, and, near a critical Nevada rail crossing, watchmen came upon two men toting sticks of dynamite. After tomatoes spattered his train in Kansas, he told his wife, "I can't go on with it anymore." When he crossed the California border, Hoover took comfort in knowing he was in his home state—but in Oakland, the terminus of the line, crowds jeered him, and on Market Street, the main artery of San Francisco, stink bombs fouled the air. By the time Hoover got to Palo Alto, he seemed to be a "walking corpse." A telegram he opened there recommended: "Vote for Roosevelt and make it unanimous."

On election night, November 8, 1932, at his home on the Stanford campus, Hoover awaited the results of the contest. One wire after another revealed that rock-ribbed Republican strongholds had turned against him. Hoover was stunned—visibly aging before his neighbors' eyes. A Palo Alto girl asked, "Mommy, what do they do to a president to make a man look like Mr. Hoover does?" Disbelieving, he clung to hope as long as he could, but when the first returns of his adopted state of California showed him trailing by half a million votes, he knew it was all over. After authorizing a concession statement, he came out from his living room to acknowledge the still-loyal Stanford students. A young women's choir sang "Taps."

. . .

No president had ever suffered so great a turnaround from his first campaign to his second. In 1928 Hoover had carried forty states; in 1932, with less than 40 percent of the popular vote, only six. Not for eighty years had there been such an avalanche of Democratic ballots. Franklin D. Roosevelt became the first Democrat to enter the White House with a popular majority since Franklin Pierce in 1853. Save for 1912, when the party divided, 1932 marked the worst defeat in the history of the GOP. The Hoover years wrenched many lifelong Republican voters from their moorings. In 1928 one couple had christened their newborn son "Herbert Hoover Jones"; four years later, they petitioned a court, "desiring to relieve the young man from the chagrin and mortification which he is suffering and will suffer," to permit his name be changed to Franklin D. Roosevelt Jones. For Hoover, election night was desolating, all the more so because it was clear that the outcome was less an affirmation of faith in FDR than a repudiation of himself. A few days later, the editor of the *Kansas City Star* found a crushed man. Hoover greeted him with a single word: "Why?"

In any other land, defeat would at least have brought surcease, but under the U.S. Constitution Hoover's ordeal in office continued for another four months—until Roosevelt's inauguration on March 4, 1933. Though the ratification in February 1933 of the Twentieth Amendment foreshortened the interregnum to January

20, it did not take effect until 1937—leaving Hoover America's last lame-duck president of the old dispensation. During his final months in office, convulsions shook the financial world; unemployment reached an awful 25 percent; and an attempt to murder the president-elect nearly succeeded. After 2,500 hunger marchers congregated on the Hill, police cordoned off the steps of the Capitol, and for the rest of the session Congress met behind a double line of rifle-bearing cops. A Pennsylvania congressman filed a twenty-four-count bill of impeachment against Hoover, and *Time* ridiculed him as "President-Reject."

In these unpropitious circumstances, Hoover moved boldly—indeed, impudently—not just to put his presidency in the most favorable light, but to undo the results of the election. The returns had hardly been counted when he invited Governor Roosevelt to collaborate on framing international economic policy. The overture appeared to indicate an extraordinarily magnanimous willingness to share authority with his successor. In fact, it was the first of a series of steps to induce Roosevelt to surrender the fruits of victory. Hoover behaved, the historian Frank Freidel later noted, "as though he felt it was his duty to save the nation, indeed the world, from the folly of the American voters."

On November 22, 1932, the president and the president-elect met in the Red Room of the White House. "The air," David Kennedy has written, "hung heavy with sullen tension." Hoover sought to put Roosevelt on record as favoring the gold standard and the president's fantasy that, by offering concessions, he could persuade Great Britain to return to the gold standard—a notion the Foreign Office called "Hoover's hare-brained scheme." Having muffed an opportunity to make progress on war debts at Lausanne earlier in the year, he also tried to rope FDR into taking a stand on that extremely unpopular issue. Throughout the discussion, Hoover adopted a condescending air toward the man the country had inexplicably chosen to replace him. Roosevelt refused to be needled. Alert as a fox who hears the baying of hounds, he smiled and smiled and smiled again, but committed himself to nothing. After the encounter was over, Hoover commented that his rival "was amiable, pleasant, anxious to be of service, very badly informed and of comparatively little vision."

For weeks, negotiations between the two men—one in Washington, the other at his ancestral home in the Hudson Valley— went nowhere, until Roosevelt asked an adviser, "Why doesn't Harry Stimson come up here and talk with me and settle this damn thing that nobody else seems able to do?" Stimson was eager to go, but Hoover, who had come to regard FDR as "a gibbering idiot," only reluctantly consented. On January 9, 1933, lines of communication were reopened when the secretary of state journeyed to Hyde Park, where he concluded that his fellow patrician was not as dim-witted as he seemed. Hoover, though, was implacable. "I will never be photographed with him," he told his press secretary. "I have too much respect for myself," adding, "I'll have my way with Roosevelt yet."

On February 17 Hoover wrote out in longhand a ten-page letter to the president-elect (whose name he misspelled "Roosvelt") catechizing him on the mounting emergency. Gold and capital were fleeing abroad, and money was being withdrawn from banks and hoarded; unemployment was rising. "The major difficulty," he asserted, "is the state of the public mind, for there is a steadily degenerating confidence in the future which has reached the height of general alarm." His policies, Hoover maintained, had pulled the country out of the depths the previous summer, but the situation had worsened since then because the country was unsettled by FDR's election, which, Hoover said, many worried might bring on radical experimentation or even "dictatorship." In short, he wanted Roosevelt to acknowledge that the country's anxiety resulted not from the failure of Hoover's policies but from apprehension about his successor. The brassy document concluded by asking Roosevelt to restore confidence through a series of statements: that "there will be no tampering or inflation of the currency; that the budget will be unquestionably balanced, even if further taxation is necessary; that the government credit will be maintained by refusal to exhaust it in the issue of securities."

Hoover knew full well what he was requesting. Three days later he confided to a conservative Pennsylvania senator that "if these declarations be made by the president-elect, he will have ratified the whole major program of the Republican Administration; that is, it means the abandonment of 90% of the so-called new deal." In a letter to another Republican senator, Hoover specified some of the proposals he expected his successor to abandon: "bills to assume Federal responsibility for billions of mortgages, loans to municipalities for public works, the Tennessee improvements and Muscle Shoals." In addition, Roosevelt must boost tariff rates and institute a national sales tax.

The letter ended whatever slim chance of cooperation remained. For days, Roosevelt—who regarded it as "cheeky"—left it unanswered. The president-elect's refusal to comply, Hoover told Stimson, was the behavior of a "madman." On March 3 Hoover, denying his successor the customary invitation to a preinaugural dinner at the White House, asked the Roosevelts for tea instead. He then marred this social occasion by again pressing his economic views and by treating the future president so cavalierly that, FDR later said, "I was sure [my son] Jimmy wanted to punch him in the eye." Roosevelt recognized, however, which man really held the upper hand. "No cosmic dramatist could possibly devise a better entrance . . . than that accorded to Franklin Delano Roosevelt," the playwright Robert Sherwood later commented. "Herbert Hoover was, in the parlance of vaudeville, 'a good act to follow.'"

Hoover could seek consolation only in knowing that his agony was nearly over. The recent session of Congress had been a nightmare. Early in 1933 both houses had overridden his veto of a bill by huge margins, forcing him to concede, "We are in a pitiful position." On his last day in office, the Washington correspondent of the *New York Times* found him "standing at the window looking out at the Washington Monument. His eyes were red; it was clear he had been weeping. We sat down and he said slowly that the country was in terrible condition, . . . that the whole economy was in jeopardy." His presidency was ending to the din of crashing banks, to the hush of silenced factory whistles. At midnight he faced up to the inevitable. "We are at the end of our string," he said. "There is nothing more we can do."

10

The Long Good-bye

Herbert Hoover did not go gently into the purgatory of the ex-presidency. He survived for another third of a century, and never in those decades did he make peace with what his countrymen had done to him. "The president was not merely rejected in November 1932," Richard Norton Smith has written. "He was virtually excommunicated." In an open touring car carrying President-elect Franklin Delano Roosevelt in an inaugural cavalcade down Pennsylvania Avenue on March 4, 1933, Hoover stared ahead stonily—refusing to respond to FDR's overtures or to the boisterous onlookers, jubilant over his ouster. Later, when his train pulled out of Union Station, he turned away from the window to conceal his tears. To a former secretary, he muttered in 1936, "Democracy is a harsh employer."

A month after his term ended, a caller found Hoover "lonely beyond measure." He could not stand being cut off from the action in Washington, where Roosevelt had launched his earthshaking First Hundred Days. At his ten-room aerie in Manhattan's Waldorf Astoria, he played solitaire or groused to anyone who would listen about that demonic FDR and those unfair journalists. He could not pick up a paper without reading how Roosevelt's dynamic leadership contrasted with his own timidity or how FDR's ready grin and cheery rhetoric inspired the nation as Hoover's despondency had

not. Instead of doing his best to ignore aspersions, Hoover sub-
scribed to a clipping service that permitted him to dwell on how
much he was detested. Not one Republican congressman, he complained, would come to his defense when the New Dealers told
outrageous lies about him. He nursed unbecoming grievances: why
had the marine band played "Hail to the Chief" on Inauguration
Day before FDR had formally taken the oath of office? Hoover
even fumed about a book by one of his former aides, though it was
patently obsequious.

Hoover did have reason to grumble, though, for he was unfairly
held responsible for both the 1929 stock market calamity and the
onset of the Great Depression. In the 1932 campaign, Roosevelt
had charged that as secretary of commerce Hoover had promoted
foreign loans, financing the speculation that brought on the crash.
It was a cheap shot. No officeholder of the era was as blameless as
Hoover for what ensued. As commerce secretary, he had issued repeated warnings against "the fever of speculation"; asked Coolidge
to prevent practices such as inside trading; and urged the Federal
Reserve to raise the discount rate in order to deter plungers in the
Great Bull Market. Worried about the "crazy and dangerous" frenzy,
he had been in the White House only two days when he exhorted
Federal Reserve officials to curb speculation. "*Please* do not use me
as a whipping boy for the 'New Era,' " Hoover implored a columnist later. "I was neither the inventor nor the promoter nor the sup-
porter of the destructive currents of that period. I was the 'receiver'
of it when it went into collapse."

Critics also misrepresented Hoover as a Wall Street lackey. "The
only trouble with capitalism is capitalists," he had told the columnist Mark Sullivan. "They're too damned greedy." Bankers were
worse than gangsters, he said. Al Capone "apparently was kind to
the poor." In 1932 Hoover had asked the Senate to investigate "sinister bear raids" on the stock exchange, and advocated legislation requiring full disclosure of stock offerings and subjecting fraudulent
promoters to punishment. "Men are not justified in deliberately
making a profit from the losses of other people," he declared. In

vain, however, did Hoover protest, "No man can foresee the coming of . . . panic. . . . I did not notice any Democratic Jeremiahs," for he had already entered national folklore as the author of the Great Depression. As a boy, the essayist Russell Baker got the straight dope from his aunt: "People were starving because of Herbert Hoover. My mother was out of work because of Herbert Hoover. Men were killing themselves because of Herbert Hoover, and their fatherless children were being packed away to orphanages . . . because of Herbert Hoover."

In the spring of 1933, the nation appeared to be breathing a collective sigh of relief. When "Who's Afraid of the Big, Bad Wolf" became a hit, psychologists explained that the song's popularity reflected national rejoicing that Hoover was no longer in the White House. "March 1933," Richard Norton Smith has noted, "cast him as black bishop to Roosevelt's white knight." For generations to come, Democrats summoned up Hoover as a specter to warn voters of the disaster that could befall the country if they elected a Republican president. Commentators have often said that FDR always ignored his actual opponents and campaigned each time against Hoover until he ran against Hitler—but even in 1944 Hoover remained a target. "We ought to be eternally grateful to Herbert Hoover, who has been our meal ticket for twelve years," a sassy New Dealer remarked.

In 1934 Secretary of the Interior Harold L. Ickes effaced the identity of the most conspicuous artifact of the Great Engineer by changing the name of Hoover Dam to Boulder Dam. "Hoover had very little to do with the dam and in fact was supposed to be opposed to it," Ickes contended. The government instructed the artist sculpting bas-reliefs on the dam to omit any mention of the former president. In response to his mean-spirited actions, Ickes, as he noted in his diary, received "a number of insulting letters," and neither the U.S. Board on Geographic Names nor Rand McNally would accept the appellation "Boulder Dam." But Ickes was pigheaded—and, with the Democrats in control, he had his way. Not until 1947 did Congress restore the structure's original name.

Hoover responded to the assaults on him, especially on his performance as president, by writing more than two dozen books—few of which served him well. When he put together *The Challenge to Liberty* (1934), expressing his rancor at Roosevelt's policies, longtime comrades in arms informed him that his writing was verbose and his views antediluvian, and counseled against publishing it. As conservative an acolyte as Robert Taft thought his treatment "extreme." But Hoover would not listen. When the *New York Times* ran a highly unfavorable review of these "brooding, bitter essays," Hoover dismissed the country's foremost newspaper as a journal that had "betrayed American institutions."

Like the deposed chief of state of a government in exile, he churned out reams of print to demonstrate that the principles he had followed were the right ones. He denied that times had been as bad as his critics were saying. Someone, he said, ought to write "a good thumping article" showing that the devastating bank crisis "really was not any great crisis after all." What others deplored as rigidity, he saw as steadfastness. At the end of 1933 he told an archconservative Republican senator, "When the American people realize some ten years hence that it was on November 8, 1932, that they surrendered the freedom of mind and spirit for which their ancestors had fought and agonized for over 300 years, they will, I hope, recollect that I at least tried to save them."

Maddened by the pretensions of the youthful New Dealers who had made their way to Washington "from the colleges mostly around Boston," Hoover lashed out in frenzied harangues. Instead of pointing out that his own officials were largely responsible for the Emergency Banking Act of March 1933 enacted under Roosevelt, he denounced this conservative (and effective) statute as a "move to gigantic socialism" bound to "raise the most appalling difficulties." FDR's farm program, he maintained, consisted of "goosestepping the people under this pinkish banner of Planned Economy." Both the National Recovery Administration and the Agricultural Adjustment Administration were "fascistic," and the Civilian Conservation Corps reminded him of an earlier effort to create a "camp of potential mercenaries . . . under sinister military leadership." The Roosevelt administration, he asserted, had "a pronounced odor of totalitarian government."

Eschewing the opportunity to dissect FDR's shortcomings deftly, Hoover spouted rhetoric even some of Roosevelt's opponents found preposterous. Critics of American individualism, he charged, had the mind-set of "those who defame the Sermon on the Mount." He went on: "They would destroy our religious faiths. Instead of a nation of self-reliant people, they would produce a nation of sycophants eating at the public trough." The New Deal, he insisted, was "a veritable fountain of fear," and the American people were in peril of becoming "pawns . . . of a self-perpetuating government." In an address to a Republican convention, he railed, "If man is merely one of the herd, Stalin is right, Hitler is right, and, God help us for our foibles and our greeds, the New Deal is right." He made no secret of his abhorrence of Roosevelt. When, at a gathering of campaign correspondents holding a down-home chicken supper, FDR's voice came on the radio, Hoover so far forgot himself that he booed the president of the United States.

Occasionally, Hoover claimed to be the fountainhead of New Deal innovations for which Roosevelt was unjustly taking credit, but much more often he presented himself as a libertarian no less resolutely opposed to government intervention than Herbert Spencer had been. On June 10, 1936, Hoover declared: "Either we shall have a society based upon ordered liberty and the initiative of the individual, or we shall have a planned society that means dictation. . . . There is no half-way ground." He continued to come across as hardhearted and divorced from the terrible suffering of the Depression. In his *Memoirs*, he ludicrously contended that during his presidency "many persons left their jobs for the more profitable one of selling apples." If a generation of historians mistakenly thought of him as an apostle of laissez-faire throughout his career, Hoover cued them to that conclusion.

His bombast had enough visceral appeal to stand-pat Republicans that, again and again, Hoover—only fifty-eight when he left office—indulged the foolish expectation that his party would seek him out as its presidential nominee. At the 1936 convention, an appeal to "recapture . . . the citadel of liberty" drew thunderous applause, interspersed with cries of "We Want Hoover!"; not even with repeated pounding of the gavel could the chairman impose order. But the delegates had no intention of going to the country with Herbert Hoover at the head of their ticket. An Ohio poll of prospective GOP voters found that he was the choice of only 4 percent.

A year later, on the day after Roosevelt announced his auda-cious scheme to pack the U.S. Supreme Court, the conservative Michigan Republican senator Arthur Vandenberg recorded in his diary: "This morning ex-president Hoover phoned me from the Waldorf-Astoria in New York eager to jump into the fray. . . . Now here is one of the tragedies of life. Hoover is still 'poison'—(the right or wrong of it does not matter). Borah, [Charles] McNary and I had a conference at 11 o'clock. Borah is prepared to lead this fight, but he insisted that there is no hope if it is trade-marked in advance as a 'Hoover fight.' . . . McNary emphatically agreed. As a matter of fact, this already was my own attitude." Affronted and seething, Hoover asked, "Who is trying to muzzle me?"

• • •

By FDR's second term, however, American eyes turned increasingly toward Europe, where the Great Humanitarian had far larger stature. In 1938, at a time when Hoover remained in low repute in his homeland, the Continent gave him a tumultuous welcome. King Leopold of Belgium decorated him, and, from Ostend to Brussels, crowds cried *"Vive l'Amérique!"* In France, the University of Lille bestowed on Hoover the first of a dozen honorary degrees; a street was named for him; and student admirers presented him with a *beret d'Honneur.*

While in Berlin on that trip, Hoover received an invitation from an astounding source: Adolf Hitler. He resolved to decline, but the U.S. ambassador urged him to meet the führer. Hoover's attitude toward the Third Reich is hard to determine. According to one account, the word *Jew* sent Hitler off on a standing tirade of several minutes. Sit down, Hoover allegedly told him. "That's enough. I'm not interested in your views." Yet Hoover permitted himself to be entertained sumptuously by Hermann Göring at his hunting lodge, and he showed no distress about the devouring of Austria. He even thought that the Nazis could improve upon the government of Czechoslovakia. On returning to America, he expressed dismay at "the heartbreaking persecution of helpless Jews," but he fretted that Jews had too much influence on U.S. foreign policy.

As Europe moved inexorably toward war in the summer of 1939, Hoover published an article to remind Americans what the Great War had been like—not a time of glory but of unspeakable terror. He wrote about soldiers in the Battle of the Somme:

> Here and there, like ants, they advanced under the thunder and belching volcanoes of 10,000 guns. Their lives were thrown away until half a million had died. Passing close by were unending lines of men plodding along the right side of the road to the front, not with drums and bands, but with saddened resignation. Down the left side came the unending lines of wounded men, staggering among unending stretchers and ambulances. . . . And it was but one battle of a hundred.

As late as mid-July, Hoover comforted himself with the conviction that Germany had no plans for aggression, certainly not against Britain or France. The main danger, he was convinced, came not from Hitler but from Roosevelt, who was discouraging the democracies from reaching an "accommodation" with Berlin. The Nazi rape of Poland in September and the outbreak of World War II neither chastened nor instructed him. In January 1940 Hoover still dismissed the thought that France might be overrun as "too impossible an event to warrant comment." In his address that year to the Republican convention in Philadelphia, he scoffed at the notion that the Fascist powers imperiled America. "Every whale that spouts is not a submarine," he said. Anyway, it would not be disastrous for the United States "if the Old World falls." But if America were to enter the war, "the last sanctuary of liberty" would disappear.

In 1940 Hoover once again believed his party's convention might deadlock and delegates would choose him as their presidential candidate. When devoted loyalists advised him to face reality, he blew up at them. Private polls, he insisted, showed "a very extraordinary turn in the tide" in his direction. He ignored a Gallup Poll that found he had the support of only 2 percent of Republicans. For a few hours, it appeared his antennae might be finer tuned than the skeptics. As his car pulled up to his Philadelphia hotel, a crowd of well-wishers chanting "Hoover! Hoover! Hoover!" was so large that it stopped traffic. When he strode down the center aisle toward the podium to speak, the band struck up "California, Here I Come," and, after he finished his warning against involvement in overseas quarrels, California delegates marched their state's standard around the hall in the hope of starting a stampede for Hoover. Almost no one joined them. The Nazi blitzkrieg through the Low Countries and France meant that neither Hoover (never seriously considered) nor the isolationist Robert Taft were viable opponents for FDR, and the party, to Hoover's dismay, settled instead for the internationalist upstart Wendell Willkie.

During the period between the convention and Pearl Harbor, Hoover saw events spin out of control. GOP leaders in Connecticut told him bluntly not to set foot in their state to campaign for the ticket because his presence would hurt the party. On the eve of the election, certain that this contest would be FDR's last hurrah, Hoover denounced the president for spewing "billingsgate" at foreign leaders, presumably Hitler in particular. He was taken aback when the American people returned Roosevelt to the White House for an unprecedented third term. Hoover opposed lend-lease and dismissed the Four Freedoms as useless without a "Fifth Freedom": free enterprise and the right "to accumulate property." But no one seemed to be listening. In December 1941 the Japanese bombs raining on Hawaii brought the United States into the global conflict he had so long striven to avert.

Hoover, who had been such a formidable figure in the Great War, sat out World War II unwanted and uncalled on. When Bernard Baruch, head of the War Industries Board in 1917, urged Roosevelt to appoint Hoover to direct economic mobilization, the president replied, "Well, I'm not Jesus Christ. I'm not going to raise him from the dead." That retort was inexcusable, and FDR has been roundly scolded for not making use of the World War I food czar's immense knowledge. But, considering Hoover's unbridled hostility toward him, it was a bit much to expect the president to take his predecessor into his official family. Moreover, the American people's bitter memories of the early years of the Great Depression made Hoover a poor choice for an administrator who would need to ask consumers to sacrifice. Furthermore, Roosevelt had, in fact, asked Hoover—through an intermediary—to come to the White House in September 1939 to advise him on how to get relief to the Poles and had been snubbed. "Hoover turned us down," Eleanor Roosevelt told a friend. "He refused to call on the President." Still, it was hard for Hoover. In January 1942 he likened himself to a "leper."

Republicans did not make his tribulation easier. At the 1944 GOP convention, Hoover's sons were shunted aside so that they would not appear in photographs with the Republican nominee, Thomas Dewey. At Wendell Willkie's funeral in October, Eleanor Roosevelt graciously went out of her way to pay her respects to Hoover, but Dewey, sitting in the same pew, pretended not to know that his party's most recent president was there. That behavior did not sit well. "Dewey has no inner reservoir of knowledge on which to draw for his thinking," Hoover confided to a friend. "A man couldn't wear a mustache like that without having it affect his mind."

A bleak year, 1944 was a time of rupture. Lou Henry Hoover, his companion since campus days, died—and with Lou, who adored their home in Palo Alto, went his most enduring bond to California. He settled in for good at what he referred to as his "comfortable monastery" on the thirty-first floor of the Waldorf Towers. The November election brought another change. After FDR's fourth victory, Hoover put his twenty-two-room Georgian mansion on S Street on the market and turned his back on Washington as a domicile forever.

. . .

No longer did anyone ask whether Hoover was a Wilsonian Democrat or a Bull Moose progressive. Rooted perdurably in the camp of GOP archconservatives after the war, he took solace in the reelection of Joe McCarthy and was gratified by the emergence of Barry Goldwater. Not even small steps by the government were tolerable. "Only a drop of typhoid in a barrel of drinking water sickens a whole village," he warned. Health insurance, he said, violated the "American way." A mission statement he prepared in 1959 for the Hoover Institution on War, Revolution and Peace—a library and conservative think tank he had founded at Stanford in 1919— lauded private enterprise and warned against federal initiatives. Liberals were disheartened by John F. Kennedy's cautious centrism, but Hoover maintained that "Kennedy's goals were evil" because they promoted "socialism disguised as a welfare state." In 1964 he told Goldwater that he would like to sell TVA, even "if I could only get a dollar for it."

By targeting progressives, Hoover reinforced the impression that he had always been a reactionary. He contended that "liberalism" was a locution "applied to those who would deny the same freedom to others which they demand for themselves—a good word turned pink inside." When he gave a televised speech at Stanford averring that "fuzzy-minded people" who were closet collectivists constituted a greater danger than Communists, the columnist I. F. Stone dismissed the talk as "the kind of chrome-plated guff which made Hoover seem a tiresome old bore before."

Given these sentiments, no one anticipated that when Hoover was recruited into public service for the first time since he was expelled from the White House, the summons would come from a

Democratic president. Less than a year after he moved into Franklin Roosevelt's chair in the Oval Office, Harry Truman began a courtship of Hoover. "He's a nice enough old man," Truman later remarked to a New Dealer, though "to the right of Louis the Fourteenth. But he deserves to be treated with respect as an ex-President. Roosevelt couldn't stand him and he hated Roosevelt. But he . . . can do some things. No reason to treat him other than with respect." Mail ran two to one against Truman's overtures to what one irate constituent called "that contemptible character, Herbert Hoover." The ex-president's name, a Philadelphia judge wrote the White House, had "a connotation that can never be erased from the memories of democratic-minded Americans—Hoovervilles, apples on the street corners, soup lines—no we want none of Mr. Hoover in any capacity." But Truman persisted, even though he thought his predecessor "doesn't understand what's happened in the world since McKinley."

"I have a job for you that nobody else in the country can do," Truman told Hoover on March 1, 1946. "You know more about feeding nations and people than anybody in the world." He wanted Hoover to take the president's private plane and fly to Europe and Asia to determine what should be done about the worldwide food crisis. Though distrustful, Hoover found the invitation irresistible. His long exile was ended. It also meant that he could enlist in a cause he cared deeply about. Even during his period of eclipse during World War II, he had raised large sums to feed the Poles and the Finns—all the while insisting that "the whole thing should be on donations from governments." Shortly after the war, he had advanced a proposal that led to the creation of the United Nations International Children's Emergency Fund (UNICEF). Moreover, he had said recently, "It is now 11:59 on the clock of starvation."

Over the next eighty-two days, the septuagenarian Hoover flew fifty thousand miles to assess the peril of famine in thirty-eight countries. "After the last war I directed food supplies for a large part of Europe," he reminded reporters in Paris. "Now I've been called back like an old family doctor." His onerous itinerary included meetings with seven kings (among them, the young monarch of Siam), the British cabinet, thirty-six prime ministers, an Indian maharaja, Pope Pius XII, and Mahatma Gandhi. When the "food ambassador" returned to the United States for a brief stopover before going on to South America, he gave a radio talk that was the most eloquent address of his life. "Hunger hangs over the homes of more than eight hundred million people—over one-third of the people of the earth," he said. "Hunger is a silent visitor who comes like a shadow. He sits beside every anxious mother three times a day. But we can save these people from the worst, if we will."

Hoover got another important assignment during the Truman presidency when in 1947 the Republican Eightieth Congress established a Commission on Organization of the Executive Branch. An autocratic chair of what became known as the "Hoover Commission," he surprised conservatives by pushing for strengthening the president's managerial capability. Though he had ranted against FDR's usurpation, he had become convinced that it was misguided for executive power to become so diffused that no one could be held accountable, especially in a nuclear age with dangerous enemies abroad. In its final report, according to the political scientist Peri Arnold, "the last Republican president joined in a celebration of the expansive, modern presidency" and the "central authority required by the majoritarian positive state."

His idiosyncratic collaboration with Truman (they have been titled "the odd couple") did not extend to foreign policy, however. Despite unparalleled prosperity, Hoover foresaw economic disaster in the willingness of the government to shoulder so large a proportion of the cost of defending the Western world. The Bretton Woods international system of monetary management, he thought, harbored "poison oak," for it reflected the giddy penchant of Americans to lend "all their money to foreigners." He had little hope for the United Nations unless it was revamped to exclude the Communist countries, and he urged the United States to "withdraw at once" from NATO, which he regarded as an exorbitant failure. When Truman fired Douglas MacArthur for insubordination,

Hoover, working through intermediaries, instructed the general to fly home immediately and then helped arrange a tumultuous welcome for him in San Francisco as well as an invitation to address Congress. He also suggested to MacArthur a theme for his oration: "The object of war is victory." Even after the frenzied exaltation of MacArthur abated, Hoover regarded him as "a reincarnation of St. Paul into a great General of the Army who came out of the East."

Hoover did not get on nearly so well with the Republican Dwight Eisenhower as he had with the Democrat Truman, however. Eisenhower honored him with an appointment to chair a second (and much more conservative) Hoover Commission on the executive branch and did all he could to cosset the former president— from inviting him on a fishing jaunt in Colorado to lionizing him on his eightieth birthday. But Hoover thought the general fell short because he would not do enough to free the government from the incubus of the New Deal. He charged that "Ike gave me a couple of left wingers" on the second Hoover Commission and had caved in to a radical cabal. "He is a very expensive president," Hoover grumbled. Still worse, Eisenhower was inept with a fly rod.

· · ·

In his final years, memories of the Great Depression dimmed, and the country increasingly came to regard Hoover as a sage, even as a national treasure. In 1957, at a banquet saluting Hoover, Senator John F. Kennedy declared: "We may say of him whom we honor tonight, as Edmund Burke said of Charles James Fox: 'He has put to hazard his ease, his security, his interest, his power, and his . . . popularity. . . . He is traduced and abused. . . . He may live long, he may do much. But . . . he can never exceed what he does this day.'" Readers swiftly made Hoover's 1958 book, *The Ordeal of Woodrow Wilson*, a surprise best seller. When he turned ninety on August 10, 1964, sixteen states proclaimed "Herbert Hoover Day."

It would be too much to say that Hoover mellowed, but he did reveal a self-deprecating, ironic wit that had not been conspicuous before. "I'm the only person of distinction," he said, "who's ever had a depression named after him." He enjoyed repeating the jest that the University Club in Manhattan was so stodgy a fellow could not take his mistress there—unless she was married to a member. When his niece revealed that she did not know how to cope with speakers who ran on and on, Hoover told her: "You just pass them up a little note and you just write on it 'your fly is open' and he'll sit down right away." Asked how he managed to endure the many years when leaders of both parties treated him as a pariah, he replied, "I outlived the bastards."

Life for a former president, Hoover remarked, came down to little save "taking pills and dedicating libraries," but he knew when he spoke that it was not true for him. Even in his last days he kept a battery of secretaries busy. On the eve of his ninetieth birthday, he was well along on yet another book. He "stayed young by working," Richard Norton Smith has written, "as well as by nurturing the animosities of a lifetime." He labored on a history of FDR and the New Deal so unbalanced that—to protect Hoover's reputation—it has been hidden away. On one occasion, asked what he was doing in the middle of the night, he retorted, "I'm making my Roosevelt book more pungent."

Hoover found little cause for joy, though, in the contemporary political scene. He recognized that Goldwater's campaign was imploding and that the country was about to return by acclamation Lyndon Baines Johnson, sponsor of the War on Poverty and the Great Society—statist programs Hoover abhorred. Prospects abroad were no better. Asked by an acquaintance bound for Europe whether there was anything he would like done, Hoover replied, "Well, you can tell the British to take their hands out of our pockets." Nearly blind, toothless, and confined to a wheelchair, he stayed feisty to the last. He was so hard of hearing that his secretaries had to shout. That was all right, Hoover told a visitor. "I'm used to being hollered at."

A little before noon on October 20, 1964, he died of an upper intestinal tract hemorrhage. Only one former president, John Adams, had lived so long. It fell to his last adversary, Lyndon Johnson, to order flags lowered to half-staff and to declare a period of thirty days of national mourning. Hoover, obituaries dutifully recorded, was almost universally judged to have been a failed president—an ineluctable reminder that the Oval Office requires more than dedication and managerial skills, both of which he had in abundance. But there was more to his career than the four years in the White House. Hoover, an associate told the press, "fed more people and saved more lives than any other man in history." On a lovely Indian summer afternoon, Herbert Hoover was interred at a site he had chosen—a grassy rise overlooking the Iowa cottage in which he had been born nine decades before.

Milestones

1874 Born in West Branch, Iowa
1884 Orphaned
1885 Sent to Oregon
1891 Enrolls at Stanford University
1895 Graduates from Stanford with bachelor of arts in geology
1896 Employed by San Francisco mining engineer Louis Janin
1897 Arrives in Australia as agent for Bewick, Moreing and Company
1899 Marries Lou Henry
       Sails to China
1901 Becomes partner in Bewick, Moreing
       Moves to London
1908 Sets up independent consulting firm
1909 Publishes *Principles of Mining*
1912 In collaboration with Lou Hoover publishes *De Re Metallica*
       Elected trustee of Stanford
1914 Organizes Committee of American Residents in London for Assistance of American Travellers
       Appointed chairman of the Commission for Relief in Belgium
1917 Appointed food administrator

1918   Heads postwar European reconstruction
1919   Maintains American Relief Administration as private operation
       Appointed vice chairman of Second Industrial Conference
1920   Announces he is a Republican
       Defeated in Republican presidential primary in California
1921   Appointed secretary of commerce by President Harding
       Sends relief to Soviet Union
1922   Publishes *American Individualism*
1927   Heads relief operation for Mississippi River flood victims
1928   Elected president of the United States
1929   Signs Agricultural Marketing Act
       Meets with British prime minister J. Ramsay MacDonald
       Convenes White House conferences to cope with the Wall Street crash and the onset of the Great Depression
1930   Signs Hawley-Smoot Tariff bill
       Establishes President's Emergency Committee for Employment
       Stresses financial prudence in State of the Union address
1931   Federal Farm Board collapses
       Mukden incident erupts in Manchuria
       Kreditanstalt fails in Austria
       Proposes moratorium on war debts and reparations
       Sets up President's Organization on Unemployment Relief
       National Credit Corporation created
1932   Stimson Doctrine enunciated
       Signs bill chartering Reconstruction Finance Corporation
       World Disarmament Conference meets in Geneva
       Signs Emergency Relief and Construction Act
       Bonus army routed
       Defeated by Franklin D. Roosevelt in presidential election
1946   Appointed food ambassador by President Truman

1947   Heads the first Hoover Commission on Organization of
        the Executive Branch
1953   Appointed chairman of the Second Hoover Commission
1964   Honored on his ninetieth birthday
        Dies in New York City

Selected Bibliography

This book draws upon more than half a century of archival research. Among the collections that proved valuable were those of William R. Castle Jr., Houghton Library, Harvard University, Cambridge, Mass.; Herbert Hoover, Herbert Hoover Presidential Library, West Branch, Iowa; Hiram Johnson, University of California, Berkeley; Alfred Landon, Kansas State Historical Society, Topeka, Kans.; George H. Moses, New Hampshire Historical Society, Concord, N.H.; William Starr Myers, Princeton University, Princeton, N.J.; Peter Norbeck, University of South Dakota, Vermillion, S.D.; John Callan O'Laughlin, Library of Congress; Franklin D. Roosevelt, Franklin D. Roosevelt Presidential Library, Hyde Park, N.Y.; Jouett Shouse, University of Kentucky, Lexington, Ky.; Henry Stimson, Yale University, New Haven, Conn.; Mark Sullivan, Hoover Institution on War, Revolution and Peace, Stanford, Calif.; Arthur Vandenberg, Michigan Historical Collections of the University of Michigan, Ann Arbor, Mich.; and Robert Wagner, Georgetown University, Washington, D.C.

BOOKS

Alchon, Guy. *The Invisible Hand of Planning: Capitalism, Social Science, and the State in the 1920s*. Princeton, N.J.: Princeton University Press, 1985.

Arnold, Peri E. *Making the Managerial Presidency: Comprehensive Reorganization Planning, 1905–1996*. Lawrence: University Press of Kansas, 1998.

Barber, William J. *From New Era to New Deal: Herbert Hoover, the Economists, and American Economic Policy, 1921–1933*. Cambridge, U.K.: Cambridge University Press, 1985.

Barry, John M. *Rising Tide: The Great Mississippi Flood of 1927 and How It Changed America*. New York: Simon and Schuster, 1997.

Bernstein, Irving. *The Lean Years: A History of the American Worker, 1920–1933*. Boston: Houghton Mifflin, 1960.

Best, Gary Dean. *Herbert Hoover, the Postpresidential Years, 1933–1964*. 2 vols. Stanford, Calif.: Hoover Institution Press, 1983.

———. *The Politics of American Individualism: Herbert Hoover in Transition, 1918–1921*. Westport, Conn.: Greenwood Press, 1975.

Brandes, Joseph. *Herbert Hoover and Economic Diplomacy: Department of Commerce Policy, 1921–1928*. Pittsburgh, Pa.: University of Pittsburgh Press, 1962.

Burner, David. *Herbert Hoover: A Public Life*. New York: Alfred A. Knopf, 1979.

———. *The Politics of Provincialism: The Democratic Party in Transition, 1918–1932*. New York: Alfred A. Knopf, 1967.

Chamberlain, Lawrence H. *The President, Congress, and Legislation*. New York: Columbia University Press, 1946.

Clements, Kendrick A. *Hoover, Conservation, and Consumerism: Engineering the Good Life*. Lawrence: University Press of Kansas, 2000.

Curry, E. R. *Hoover's Dominican Diplomacy and the Origins of the Good Neighbor Policy*. New York: Garland, 1979.

Daniels, Roger. *The Bonus March: An Episode of the Great Depression*. Westport, Conn.: Greenwood, 1971.

DeConde, Alexander. *Herbert Hoover's Latin-American Policy*. New York: Octagon Books, 1970.

Dozer, Donald Marquand. *Are We Good Neighbors? Three Decades of Inter-American Relations, 1930–1960*. Gainesville: University of Florida Press, 1959.

Eckley, Wilton. *Herbert Hoover*. Boston: Twayne, 1980.

Ellis, L. Ethan. *Republican Foreign Policy, 1921–1933*. New Brunswick, N.J.: Rutgers University Press, 1968.

Fausold, Martin L. *The Presidency of Herbert C. Hoover*. Lawrence: University Press of Kansas, 1985.

———, and George T. Mazuzan, eds. *The Hoover Presidency: A Reappraisal*. Albany: State University of New York Press, 1974.

Ferrell, Robert H. *American Diplomacy in the Great Depression: Hoover-Stimson Foreign Policy, 1929–1933*. New Haven, Conn.: Yale University Press, 1957.

Gaddis, Vincent H. *Herbert Hoover, Unemployment, and the Public Sphere: A Conceptual History, 1919–1933*. Lanham, Md.: University Press of America, 2005.

Galbraith, John Kenneth. *The Great Crash: 1929*. Boston: Houghton Mifflin, 1955.

Gelfand, Lawrence E., ed. *Herbert Hoover: The Great War and Its Aftermath, 1914–23.* Iowa City: University of Iowa Press, 1979.

Gilbert, Clinton. *The Mirrors of Washington . . . with Fourteen Cartoons by Cesare and Fourteen Portraits.* New York: G. P. Putnam's Sons, 1921.

Hamilton, David E. *From New Day to New Deal: American Farm Policy from Hoover to Roosevelt, 1928–1933.* Chapel Hill: University of North Carolina Press, 1991.

Hawley, Ellis W., ed. *Herbert Hoover as Secretary of Commerce: Studies in New Era Thought and Practice.* Iowa City: University Press of Iowa, 1981.

————, et al. *Herbert Hoover and the Crisis of American Capitalism.* Cambridge, Mass.: Schenkman, 1973.

————, et al. *Herbert Hoover and the Historians.* West Branch, Iowa: Herbert Hoover Presidential Association, 1989.

Hoff, Joan. *American Business and Foreign Policy, 1920–1933.* Lexington: University Press of Kentucky, 1971.

————. *Herbert Hoover: Forgotten Progressive.* Boston: Little Brown, 1975.

Hofstadter, Richard. *The American Political Tradition and the Men Who Made It.* New York: Alfred A. Knopf, 1948.

Hoover, Herbert. *American Individualism.* Garden City, N.Y.: Doubleday, Page, 1923.

————. *Memoirs.* 3 vols. New York: Macmillan, 1951, 1952.

Huthmacher, J. Joseph. *Senator Robert F. Wagner and the Rise of Urban Liberalism.* New York: Atheneum, 1968.

Irwin, Will. *Herbert Hoover: A Reminiscent Biography.* New York: Century, 1928.

Joslin, Theodore. *Hoover Off the Record.* Garden City, N.Y.: Doubleday, Doran, 1934.

Kellogg, Vernon. *Herbert Hoover: The Man and His Work.* New York: D. Appleton, 1920.

Kelly, Lawrence C. *The Navajo Indians and Federal Indian Policy, 1900–1935.* Tucson: University of Arizona Press, 1968.

Kennedy, David M. *Freedom from Fear: The American People in Depression and War, 1929–1945.* New York: Oxford University Press, 1999.

Krog, Carl E., and William R. Tanner, eds. *Herbert Hoover and the Republican Era: A Reconsideration.* Lanham, Md.: University Press of America, 1984.

Leach, William. *Land of Desire: Merchants, Power, and the Rise of a New American Culture.* New York: Pantheon, 1993.

Leffler, Melvyn P. *The Elusive Quest: America's Pursuit of European Stability and French Security, 1919–1933.* Chapel Hill: University of North Carolina Press, 1979.

Leuchtenburg, William E. *Franklin D. Roosevelt and the New Deal, 1932–1940.* New York: Harper and Row, 1963.

———. *The Perils of Prosperity, 1914–1932.* Chicago: University of Chicago Press, 1958. Second edition, 1993.

Lichtman, Allan J. *Prejudice and the Old Politics: The Presidential Election of 1928.* Chapel Hill: University of North Carolina Press, 1979.

Liebovich, Louis W. *Bylines in Despair: Herbert Hoover, the Great Depression, and the U.S. News Media.* Westport, Conn.: Praeger, 1991.

Lisio, Donald J. *Hoover, Blacks, and Lily-Whites: A Study of Southern Strategies.* Chapel Hill: University of North Carolina Press, 1985.

———. *The President and Protest: Hoover, Conspiracy, and the Bonus Riot.* Columbia: University of Missouri Press, 1974.

Lloyd, Craig. *Aggressive Introvert: A Study of Herbert Hoover and Public Relations Management, 1912–1932.* Columbus: Ohio State University Press, 1972.

Lowitt, Richard. *George W. Norris: The Persistence of a Progressive, 1913–1933.* Urbana: University of Illinois Press, 1971.

Lyons, Eugene. *Our Unknown Ex-President: A Portrait of Herbert Hoover.* Garden City, N.Y.: Doubleday, 1948.

McCoy, Donald R. *Calvin Coolidge: The Quiet President.* New York: Macmillan, 1967.

Moore, Edmund A. *A Catholic Runs for President: The Campaign of 1928.* New York: Ronald Press, 1956.

Mullendore, William Clinton. *History of the United States Food Administration, 1917–1919.* Stanford, Calif.: Stanford University Press, 1941.

Murray, Robert K. *Warren G. Harding and His Administration.* Minneapolis: University of Minnesota Press, 1969.

Myers, William Starr, ed. *State Papers and Other Public Writings of Herbert Hoover.* Garden City, N.Y.: Doubleday Doran, 1934.

———, and Walter H. Newton. *The Hoover Administration: A Documented Narrative.* New York: Charles Scribner and Sons, 1936.

Nash, George H. *Herbert Hoover and Stanford University.* Stanford, Calif.: Hoover Institution Press, 1988.

———. *The Life of Herbert Hoover.* 3 vols. New York: W. W. Norton, 1983–1996.

Nash, Gerald D. *United States Oil Policy 1890–1964: Business and Government in Twentieth-Century America.* Pittsburgh, Pa.: University of Pittsburgh Press, 1968.

Nash, Lee, ed. *Understanding Herbert Hoover: Ten Perspectives.* Stanford, Calif.: Hoover Institution Press, 1987.

Olson, James Stuart. *Herbert Hoover and the Reconstruction Finance Corporation, 1931–1933.* Ames: Iowa State University Press, 1977.

Pollard, James E. *The Presidents and the Press*. New York: Macmillan, 1947.

Public Papers of the Presidents: Herbert Hoover, Containing the Public Messages, Speeches and Statements of the President. 6 vols. Washington, D.C.: Government Printing Office, 1974–76.

Robinson, Edgar Eugene, and Vaughn Davis Bornet. *Herbert Hoover: President of the United States*. Stanford, Calif.: Hoover Institution Press, 1975.

Rosen, Elliot A. *Hoover, Roosevelt, and the Brains Trust: From Depression to New Deal*. New York: Columbia University Press, 1977.

Schlesinger, Arthur M., Jr. *The Crisis of the Old Order, 1919–1933*. Boston: Houghton Mifflin, 1957.

Schmitz, David F. *Henry L. Stimson: The First Wise Man*. Wilmington, Del.: Scholarly Resources, 2001.

Smith, Gene. *The Shattered Dream: Herbert Hoover and the Great Depression*. New York: William Morrow, 1970.

Smith, Richard Norton. *An Uncommon Man: The Triumph of Herbert Hoover*. New York: Simon and Schuster, 1984.

Sobel, Robert. *Herbert Hoover at the Onset of the Great Depression, 1929–1930*. Philadelphia, Pa.: J. B. Lippincott, 1975.

Swain, Donald C. *Federal Conservation Policy, 1921–1933*. Berkeley and Los Angeles: University of California Press, 1963.

———. *Wilderness Defender: Horace M. Albright and Conservation*. Chicago: University of Chicago Press, 1970.

Walch, Timothy, ed. *Uncommon Americans: The Lives and Legacies of Herbert and Lou Henry Hoover*. Westport, Conn.: Praeger, 2003.

———, and Dwight M. Miller. *Herbert Hoover and Franklin D. Roosevelt: A Documentary History*. Westport, Conn.: Greenwood Press, 1998.

———. *Herbert Hoover and Harry S. Truman: A Documentary History*. Worland, Wyo.: High Plains Publishing Company, 1992.

Warren, Harris Gaylord. *Herbert Hoover and the Great Depression*. New York: Oxford University Press, 1959.

Weed, Clyde P. *The Nemesis of Reform: The Republican Party During the New Deal*. New York: Columbia University Press, 1994.

Wert, Hal Elliott. *Hoover, the Fishing President: Portrait of the Private Man and His Life Outdoors*. Mechanicsburg, Pa.: Stackpole Books, 2005.

Wilbur, Ray Lyman. *Memoirs, 1875–1949*, ed. Edgar Eugene Robinson and Paul Carroll Edwards. Stanford, Calif.: Stanford University Press, 1960.

———, and Arthur Mastick Hyde. *The Hoover Policies*. New York: Charles Scribner's Sons, 1937.

Wood, Bryce. *The Making of the Good Neighbor Policy.* New York: Columbia University Press, 1961.

Young, Nancy Beck. *Lou Henry Hoover: Activist First Lady.* Lawrence: University Press of Kansas, 2004.

Zieger, Robert H. *Republicans and Labor, 1919–1929.* Lexington: University of Kentucky Press, 1969.

Acknowledgments

By far my greatest debt, once again, is to my wife, Jean Anne, who makes writing a merry adventure and who brings to editing the skills honed as a writing instructor at universities in Texas and Ohio and as director of publications at the National Humanities Center. No words of mine can convey how much she has given and goes on giving.

At Times Books, the late Arthur M. Schlesinger Jr. invited me to write this volume. We were friends for sixty years, and I am saddened that he is not here to scrutinize the book he commissioned. His successor, Sean Wilentz, made a number of helpful suggestions, and senior editor Robin Dennis devoted an extraordinary amount of attention to a close and acute reading of the manuscript.

I also am grateful to the corps of revisionist historians who have labored indefatigably to provide us with a more nuanced portrait of Hoover than we have ever had before and to the staff of the Herbert Hoover Presidential Library who have made that possible.

Index

ABOUT THE AUTHOR

WILLIAM E. LEUCHTENBURG, professor emeritus at the University of North Carolina at Chapel Hill, is a noted authority on twentieth-century American history. Winner of both the Bancroft and Parkman prizes, he is the author of more than a dozen books. A Guggenheim Fellow and a Mellon Senior Fellow, he has been elected president of both the American Historical Association and the Organization of American Historians. In 2008, he was chosen as the first recipient of the Arthur M. Schlesinger Jr. Award for Distinguished Writing in American History of Enduring Public Significance.